sunil Gavaskar

STRAIGHT Drive

AF148649

STRAIGHT *Drive*

Sunil Manohar Gavaskar (b. 10 July 1949) was brought up in Mumbai where he attended St. Xavier's High School and St. Xavier's College. He inherited his interest in cricket from his parents and uncle and justified their high hopes when, in 1961, at the age of twelve, he distinguished himself in inter-school tournaments. The College XI, the Irani Cup and the Ranji Trophy paved the way for selection in Test cricket. In 1971, Gavaskar made his debut in the West Indies where he scored an astounding 774 runs in 4 Tests at an average of 154.8. With 34 Test centuries to his credit, Gavaskar surpassed Donald Bradman's thirty-five-year-old record of 29 Test centuries. He has played 125 Test matches scoring 10,122 runs; 108 One-Day matches and scored 3,092 runs and holds the distinction of captaining India in 47 Tests. Gavaskar has been felicitated with the Arjuna Award in 1975, Padma Bhushan in 1980, and the Maharashtra Bhushan Award in 1999.

Gavaskar is also a TV commentator for Sharjah, BBC, Channel 9 Network, ESPN Star Sports and Neo Sports. He has held several important posts including that of chairman of ICC Cricket Committee, National Cricket Committee and the BCCI Technical Committee. He also has to his credit four books including *Sunny Days* (1976), *Idols* (1983), *Runs 'n' Ruins* (1984) and *One Day Wonders* (1985).

STRAIGHT *Drive*

Sunil Gavaskar

Rupa & Co

Copyright © Sunil Gavaskar 2009

First Published 2009
First in Rupa Paperback 2011

Published by
Rupa Publications India Pvt. Ltd.
7/16, Ansari Road, Daryaganj,
New Delhi 110 002

Sales Centres:
Allahabad Bengaluru Chennai
Hyderabad Jaipur Kathmandu
Kolkata Mumbai

All rights reserved.
No part of this publication may be reproduced,
stored in a retrieval system, or transmitted,
in any form or by any means, electronic,
mechanical, photocopying, recording or otherwise,
without the prior permission of the publishers.

The author asserts the moral right to be
identified as the author of this work.

Photo credits:
Rupa & Co. would like to thank the MiD DAY Group of
Publications, Professional management Group and the
author etc. for the use of photographs. Several have been
sourced from the existing Rupa & Co. Archives

Cover and book design:
PealiDezine, D4/4232, Vasant Kunj, New Delhi 110 070

Printed in India by
Nutech Photolithographers, New Delhi 110 020

At the lotus feet of
Bhagwan Sri Sathya Sai Baba

CONTENTS

ACKNOWLEDGEMENTS

Aajkaal, Kolkata

Arab News, Jeddah

Dainik Jagran, Kanpur

Eenadu, Hyderabad

Emirates Today, Dubai

Gomantak Times, Goa

Gujarat Mitra, Surat

Gujarat Samachar, Ahmedabad

Gujarati MiD DAY, Mumbai

Gulf News, Dubai

Hindustan Times, New Delhi

Hitavada, Nagpur

Mahanagar, Mumbai

MiD DAY, Mumbai

Sakal Times, Pune

The Telegraph, Kolkata

The Happy 'Gavaskar' Family

FOREWORD

Many years have passed since Sunil's first ever book *Sunny Days* was published in 1976 and welcomed by the sports loving public. Since then we always toyed with the suggestion that Sunil wrote a 'sequel' narrating further progress in career in his own inimitable style. We broached the subject to him a few times but there was no real enthusiastic response.

Writing, especially an autobiography, is an impulsive passion which requires an appropriate environment. Sunil's sights were then on television commentary which had just commenced in India on the arrival and progress of satellite television in general. He got fully immersed in it and thoroughly enjoyed it, and still does.

Despite this little diversion, however, his main passion at heart for writing continued in the shape of columns on the various sporting events. Over these years, more than 600 columns have been published in many regional national and international newspapers and magazines, appreciated by the sporting public for his frank and witty appraisal of the events.

Quite a number of biographies have been written on his achievements but not his own after *Sunny Days*.

When we celebrated our own sixty-first wedding anniversary last year, this suggestion surged in our minds once again and with his consent we decided to publish a book containing sixty-one selected columns written over a period to coincide with his 'Sixty-First' birthday.

The selection is an appreciative, emotional, and instructive appraisal of the persons and events around him now that he also reaches his own milestone, 'Sixty' on 10 July 2009.

A Very Happy Birthday to you, dear Sunil.

Hope you all will enjoy reading this.

Aai and Baba

PREFACE

I love writing. Perhaps even more than I loved batting. I love reading too though as the eyes start to dim the reading is restricted considerably. During a Test match I would be able to finish two novels easily especially if I got out early.

Though the reading has become less, the writing has increased. There is not the slightest doubt in my mind that I am writing too much but then I really do enjoy it.

I write from the heart; very, very seldom with the head and that's why I get into controversies. Incidents, people, happenings, personalities, which could have been worded differently if I had used my head instead of my heart, would not have offended. It has never been personal though but only the love of the game and my country which makes me write what comes out strongly because I feel strongly about it. I have never been afraid of repercussions simply because I am not interested in positions nor looking for favours and besides it would have curbed my writing.

What I have curbed is the instinct to write a book after *One-Day Wonders*. Friends and family have tried to persuade me to complete my autobiography after *Sunny Days*. That and the other books were controversial because they were honest and any autobiography which is honest is bound to generate controversy and I am getting to the age where I don't want any controversies if I can avoid it. I get enough when I write a strong column.

My parents wanted me to bring out another book. So here it is. All the columns have been selected by my dear father. He loved them when they were written then and felt they should be read again by those who may have missed out when they first appeared years ago.

That's *Straight Drive* for you.

Sunil Gavaskar

issue:
badminton
..., Prakash
...ove; Courts at the
...gland Badminton
...onship; Former
...ion champion
... Frost

ALL CLASS at All England

What a fantastic tournament the All England Badminton was! For a first-time visitor, there was everything right from the efficiency in organising invitations, press cards and of course, the fabulous badminton. There were upsets galore in the singles and the Chinese men feared so much were nowhere in the last four. In the ladies singles, the reigning champion as well as the previous year's champion was dethroned and a new one installed. The best part, however, was the doubles, whether men's, ladies or mixed. The action was so fast and non-stop that if one blinked then there was the danger of missing a shot.

On the first day, there were six courts instead of seven that used to be the norm till last year. This year, there was some kind of a stage show prior to the badminton where the seats had been brought into the playing arena and thus the courts were down to six and in a completely different direction than the previous year. This naturally brought forth howls of protests from the regulars who have been watching the event unfailingly every year. They buy the same reserved seats too every year and thus the change of courts did affect them and no wonder they protested. On the first couple of days there were six courts and since they were facing each other, I wondered how the movement on the other court did not disturb the players. There was quite a bit of movement from the spectators' gallery, particularly the seats next to the courts, but the play went on regardless. By the second day, Indian challenge had unfortunately ended but to the Indian players' credit, they fought every inch of the way. After their loss they spent their time watching the other matches on the next three days and hopefully, they observed enough to help them in their future matches. As the days progressed, the number of courts declined so that on the third day there were three, on the fourth day there were two and on the final day there was just one court.

The ladies singles final was to all purposes a no contest as the Chinese girl Gu Jiaming beat the Korean girl Lee Young Suk quite easily, the match barely lasting a quarter of an hour. The men's final was a different story, however, as Morten Frost was surprisingly beaten by the younger Ib Frederiksen in three games... Frost captured the first one easily and looked good in the second till Frederiksen engaged him in big rallies. Suddenly Frost looked a little slow and a little tired and it was no surprise when Frederiksen took the second game. The five-minute break we thought was good enough for Frost to recover and come roaring back. Prakash, who I was fortunate to be sitting beside, was quite certain that Frost's experience would stand by him in the decider. We were having a snack of sorts and when we went in after hearing some applause, we were shocked to see that Frederiksen was leading 8-0. Prakash mentioned that Frederiksen should not try to finish off the match but should play a normal game. Instead Frederiksen tried to finish off earlier and played into Frost's hands. Frost levelled the score eight all and even went a point ahead and now looked stronger and confident. Frederiksen, however, pulled himself out of the rut he was falling in and took a grip on himself and when he went to match point there was a hush that made more noise than any applause court. After a short rally, he smashed the winning point and tossed the racket in the air and went for a walkabout with his face held in his hand. When Frost found him squatting on the floor with his face in his hands, he gently patted him on the back, raised him and put an arm around him. What a gesture that was! A touching moment as one champion gave his crown to the other.

The men's doubles thereafter was a bit like a pair of West Indies fast bowlers bowling to each other. The speed and the power were incredible. When one side stopped smashing, the other started. All one could do was to shake one's head in admiration for the fitness of these players and their remarkable stamina. Fortunately, the television showed highlights of the finals for two days and thus one could record the events of those days and see it at leisure whenever one wants to see non-stop action. Surprisingly this event was not covered live by the television though it has become one of the richest sporting events with pound sterling 70,000 offered as prize money.

News has just come in as this is being written that India has entered the finals of the Sharjah tournament by beating New Zealand by a convincing margin. One is thus in a happier frame of mind as one enplanes for Sharjah as an invitee of Abdul Rehman Bukhatir. It'll be different going to Sharjah to watch instead of playing there but when the team takes the field on Friday, I am sure my heart will beat a little faster. It was good to hear Mohinder Amarnath do well and score a century and get yet another man of the match award. This is his benefit year as well since he is going to be honoured along with his legendary father at the end of the tournament. Every time 'Jimbo' does well, there is a special pleasure. Since we have played together from school days, we go back a long way. If only somehow 'Jimbo' captains India in an official Test, it'll be the icing on the cake for him. India has no

With Prakash Padukone.

finer servant than 'Jimbo' and one can only take one's hat off to him and say more power to your legs, 'Jimbo'.

This year is also the Golden Jubilee year of Tata Sports Club and they are celebrating it with three major sporting events of which two are already over. One was an All-India Snooker Invitational Tourney and the other was an All-India Athletics event in Jamshedpur. The third one is going to be a cricket game between Tatas XI and the Rest XI to be played on 3 April at the Wankhede stadium. The House of Tatas have done the country proud not only in their respective fields but also in the field of sports. They were among the first to start employing sports persons so that during their active sporting days the person could participate without worrying about making the ends meet and after his sporting career was over, he could make a career in the organisation. Thus thousands of sports persons are indebted to the House of Tatas. It is therefore an honour to be asked to play in the cricket game to commemorate the golden jubilee of their sports club. I do hope more such far-thinking organisations come up to help sports persons of the country and if one may be permitted, on behalf of the sporting fraternity, a big congratulations to the sports club and thank you to the House of Tatas.

30.03.1988

right:
Patil, Kapil Dev

CHARITY BEGINS at Home

With the completion of the two charity matches in Coimbatore and Madurai last week, the Indian cricket season, at least as far as the Test cricketers are concerned, seems to be over.

Sure there will be a tourney or two in some part of the country. But the Test cricketers will not be playing in it because most of the top ones are out of the country or will be going out in a short while. That should give the non-recognised cricketers the chance to show their abilities because not much cricket will be in the news and their efforts will get highlighted and people will come to know of them. The more good cricketers there are the better the competition for the places and thus the standard of the game will become higher.

Lots of people scoff at the charity matches that are played saying that this is just another method of making a fast buck. What these people do not seem to understand is that most of these matches are played in the smaller centres. The message of the game spreads there too. When the top players play in these centres, it inspires the youngsters in the area to emulate their heroes which in turn might mean that there is the possibility of a top player coming on from the area. Look at Chandigarh. After Kapil, the place has given a few more Test cricketers to the country and looks set to give a few more. All solely due to the presence of Kapil. The crowds at these games thoroughly enjoy themselves and get to see good cricket if the wicket is good and the two teams are well-matched. The players also, free from the tensions and pressures of international cricket, play refreshingly bright cricket, establish a super rapport with the crowd and have fun which they cannot have in the grim arena of Test and One-day cricket. But, for this to happen, the most important ingredient is a good wicket. If the wicket behaves then cricket is invariably serious. True, nobody tries to knock each other's heads off with bouncers and nobody tries to run too many sharp singles and twos. The bowlers are the ones who suffer because the deliveries which one would think twice before playing in a competitive game are despatched without fear to the boundary or over. Hardly a ball goes by without something happening. Earlier, charity and benefit games were more of the donkey-drop variety but nowadays they are played seriously and the only fooling that goes on is normally in the last few overs when the non-regular bowlers bowl mainly on the crowd's demand. Thus the twin purposes of helping the charity and entertaining the crowds are well served and if there are cynics around who still call these matches just another way to make money all-round, then the only answer is that these are the very people who seldom, if ever, even touch their own purses when it comes to contributing to charities or benefits. All they contribute is a lot of words, and empty words at that.

While the Indian season is thus over for the country's superstars, another one has begun for them in other countries. Most of the younger lot of Test players have made the annual trip to England to play in the leagues of Lancashire, Yorkshire, Scotland or Ireland. The cricket at these places, though not of high standard, is very competitive and played very hard and on the professional side, the player has to bear the burden of being the batsman, bowler as well as the tactician even if somebody else is the captain. As a pro he is also expected to coach the younger members of the club or the children of the members on weekdays. So it is not exactly a holiday as one would like to believe, yet the experience of staying on one's own without the protected environment at home can toughen up a player considerably. Of course, it can also lead one astray but then it all depends on one's temperament and attitude towards the game.

There are lots of teams that go on various tours and most of the members of such teams come back with loads of goodies but very little experience of cricket. One team that looks like getting out of the rut and going on a real cricket tour is the team of under-19 players that Kailash Gattani is taking to England in early June. During his playing days Kailash was a dedicated player who, if born later, would have certainly played for India. Unfortunately, he was around when spin was the king and thus could not get a look-in, in spite of being probably the best new-ball bowler of that time in the country. He played a lot in the leagues and with the contacts he has built up there he has been able to arrange over 20 matches at various places. The players he is taking are all under-19 and most of them are knocking on the doors of first-class cricket. Most of the youngsters have been either sponsored or are bringing advertising support to pay for their fare. The trust formed by Mrs. Poddar in Calcutta for the benefit and welfare of young cricketers is sponsoring two cricketers in Gattani's team, one of whom is the schoolboy wonder Sachin Tendulkar. If the weather is good, then the youngsters should have a great experience of English Cricket and while they are there, they will get the chance to see some Test cricket between England and West Indies albeit on the television screen. With Kailash on hand and national selector Raj Singh an absolute fanatical cricket lover also in England to give them a guiding hand, the tour should be memorable for the youngsters.

The other important tour taking place is to East Africa. This team organised by Bharat Reddy and led by Kapil Dev, and consisting of some of the most promising youngsters in the country should be worth following, because as always the East Africans will be trying to impress the authorities that they are good enough to be taken seriously for future tours, preferably official ones. They have had some good players in the past and if the political upheavals in their countries in the recent past have not affected them, then they are bound to have some good players on show. For Kapil, it will be going back to the place where he made such a tremendous impact

Kapil at his best with the bat.

ten years ago, an impact that propelled him towards the Indian cap later that year. The tour also assumes importance because East Africa has now become the place where our cricketers have started to go instead of the leagues in England. This trend was started by Sandeep Patil and it is under his guidance and initiative that some more cricketers will be going to play club cricket in East Africa. So, instead of wasting their time doing nothing while it pours over most of India, our young players will be gainfully employed and keeping in touch with the game which is so important at the international level today.

11.05.1988

VIJAY WILL ALWAYS be Vijay

Vijay Amritraj is in the news again. Not that he was ever out of it but this time the news is unflattering, which is surprising for, by and large, Vijay has always had good press. He is one of those top sportspersons truly liked by the media. Of course the odd critic is bound to be there but that's always a good thing because it keeps one on one's toes. However, this time after the All India Tennis Association (A.I.T.A.) meeting, it appears that the entire press corps is up in arms against Vijay and making allegations on the basis of what transpired at the A.I.T.A. meeting. Among the things Vijay is accused of, besides making money, is a dictatorial attitude towards team selection, and the choice of venues and the choice of a coach.

The biggest accusation concerns Vijay's attitude towards his brother Anand. Vijay's insistence that he and Anand are still the best doubles pair in the country is being disputed. The easiest way to solve this is to ask Vijay and Anand to play against the other top-rated combinations in the country. In any sport, captains tend to rely on players in whom they have confidence. Sometimes this confidence can be misplaced and precisely for that there are selection committees to discuss the merits of other players, and the committee sits with the captain and chalks out the combination likely to bring success.

It is the same with venues. The captain needs to be consulted about the venue that will best suit the team and here also the selection committee can combine with the captain. These are certainly not areas of conflict but of co-operation for the benefit of Indian tennis.

As for the coach, Vijay perhaps feels that Gene Malin is more conversant with the latest methods and tactics and knows the players since he has been with them for some time now. This again can be sorted out by discussions across the table. Vijay is an extremely reasonable person and there is no need to take an attitude of confrontation for anybody. In fact, in Indian sport, the moment a top player starts to slide, the officials try to get into a position where the slide is hurried, not halted and Vijay today finds himself in that position. The attitude of the officials is bold today because they feel that Vijay is not at his peak and hence vulnerable. What they fail to understand is that the glory Vijay has brought to Indian tennis is more than

Vijay Amritraj with his young fans.

what their contribution is ever going to be. So, instead of trying to push Vijay down, they should get together with him and chalk out what will be beneficial for the future of Indian tennis.

Finally, to the financial aspect of the whole episode. Reports of the A.I.T.A. meeting reveal that Vijay and Anand Amritraj are due approximately Rs 7 lakh each for the 6 matches they played in Davis Cup (the cricket baiters should surely be stumped by this figure for don't they always moan that cricketers are the highest paid sportspersons). This figure represents twenty percent each of the funds that the A.I.T.A. gets for the Davis Cup. If this is the agreed amount by the secretary and the players, then there is no point blaming Vijay because he is only asking for what is due to him and his brother. If proper sanctions were not obtained, then it is the official who should be blamed and not the player. By trying to blame Vijay, the officials are up to their usual trick of shielding themselves by passing the buck on to the players.

All things considered, it does appear that the allegations against Vijay are just a method by the new set of officials of showing their strength. By trying to show Vijay up in poor light, they are hoping to get sympathy for their actions. But Vijay will always be Vijay. Not just a superb tennis player but a magnificent ambassador for the country and the game of tennis. And it is in the interest of Indian tennis that the officials and players sit across the table and sort out their differences rather than using the media as a platform to score moral points.

While the media has lapped up the controversy gleefully, it has to a large extent neglected the under-19 cricket tour of Pakistan. Except for a paper in the south which regularly reports the scores, most other papers do not even give a line to the tour. These are the youngsters on whom our future cricketing hopes depend to a great extent and they are being ignored by the media while a controversy which will not help Indian tennis is sought to be highlighted. If controversy is what the media wants, then they could check out who finally went as a replacement for one of the under-19 boys who came back after being ill. The chairman of the under-19 Selection Committee wanted a player from his state to go as a replacement while the manager of the team wanted a player from his state. All this while the regular stand-by (not from either state) was selected when the tour party was announced. So who finally went, if anybody went at all? And if the above information is wrong, then I will be happy to stand corrected.

The MRF pace foundation must have had mixed emotions when the Indian team was announced. T.A. Sekhar who is one of the coaches was in the running for a place in the side and his selection would have been an indirect boost to the MRF pace foundation though what they would really like is for one of their batches to don the India cap successfully. But there must also be relief at Sekhar's omission because with Dennis Lillee making sporadic appearances and Venkat, the director of coaching going away for three months as manager of the Indian team, Sekhar was the only person left to look after the boys at the foundation. If Sekhar had been picked, then the foundation would have been without direction for over three months and that is not an ideal situation. Sekhar should have gone on the 1983 tour because in his appearances in Pakistan as replacement for the injured Madan Lal, he had made the Pakistani batsmen hurry their shots. But what happened? Sekhar was left out and Madan taken on tour wrapped in cotton wool because he had still not recovered from the operation on his heel. If memory serves me right, Madan Lal played his first match only after the first couple of Tests were over, so for almost half the tour he was only a tourist. So Sekhar, who was dubbed then as injury-prone, was left behind in Madras while a player recovering from injury made the trip. The media did not utter a word because the honeymoon with the new captain was on.

You see, in our country, the media is allowed to play its favourites but Vijay Amritraj isn't!

16.02.1989

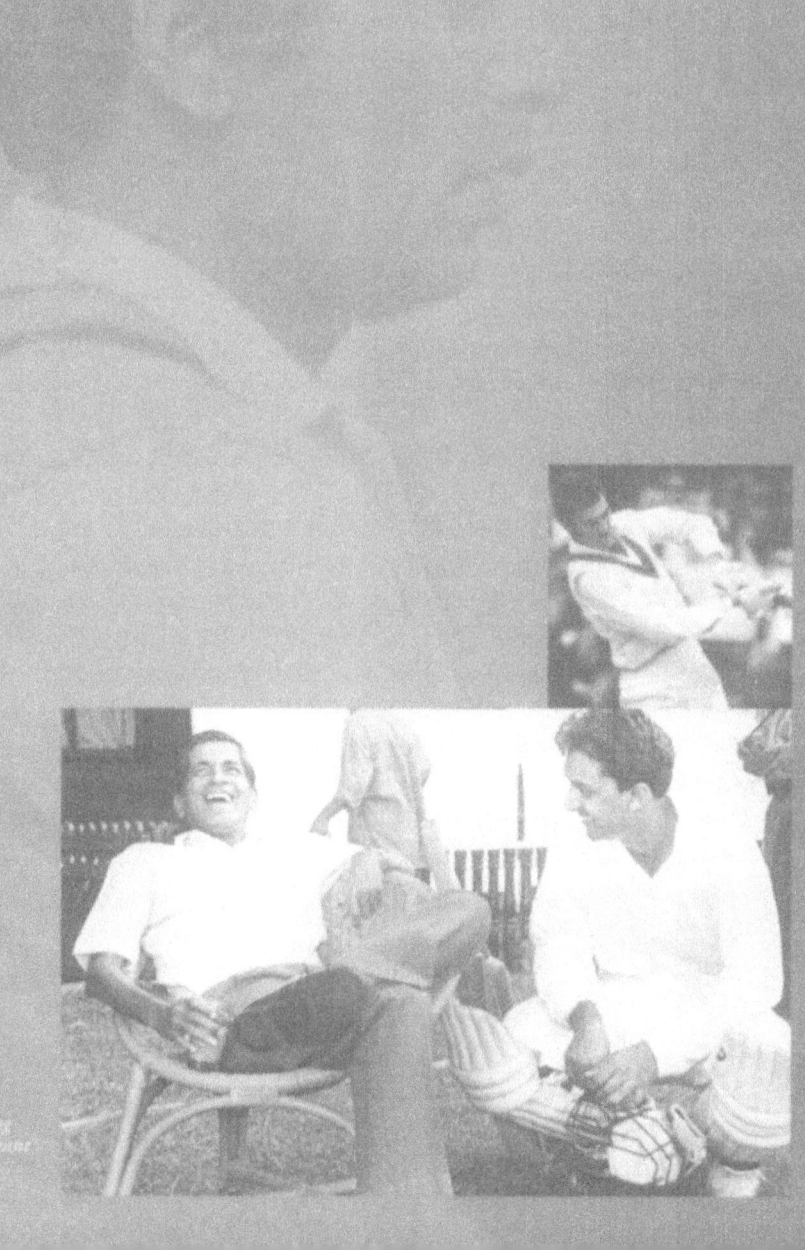

*...hossmu
...appell showing
...play: Ramakant
...di Rahen*

RAMAKANT, KARSAN...
Those Two Pals of Mine

First things first, the BCCI needs to be congratulated for allowing the Indian cricket team to participate in the benefit of two extremely well-liked cricketers, Karsan Ghavri and Ramakant Desai. For Ghavri's match, the players took leave from the camp and travelled all the way to Rajkot, and for Ramakant Desai's game, they played with barely a few hours left for their departure to the West Indies.

While Ghavri's match did not attract the expected crowds, the Desai game was well attended. Ghavri opened the bowling with Desai for ACC just when Desai was finished with first class cricket. Karsan was one of the most under-rated cricketers and he seldom got the recognition that was due to him. In the mid 1970s, he was a terror on the domestic circuit and with Madan Lal, he was the most popular player in Bombay. With over a hundred Test wickets and over 900 runs, he came close to achieving the double, but was fading rapidly when he was dropped. Apart from his new-ball bowling, he was more than a useful spinner but never really got the long bowl that he needed because spinners those days were supposed to give the ball air on all surfaces and anybody who did not was not considered good enough. Karsan's bouncer was his most lethal ball, because it was seldom wasted. Also, because he bowled left arm over the wicket, the angle of the bouncer was such that if the batman missed, then he would be hit. It was after Mike Brearley was hit, in spite of a visor, that the British press raised doubts over the legality of his action, and then all the slow motion replays showed that Karsan's action was clean as a whistle. This noise about his action was made again in the following year in Australia after he hit Greg Chappel on the head in the One-day game. The ball went off Greg's head for leg byes which incidentally were the winning runs for Australia. As we raced back to the pavilion Greg said to me, 'I don't mind how many bouncers Karsan bowls, so long as he does not chuck 'em.' I told him, 'You take care of Lenny (Pascoe) and I will take care of Karsan.' From that moment onwards, and also possibly because I did not support him in condemning the Melbourne pitch, Greg turned cool towards me for the rest of the season.

In Ramakant's case too, doubts were raised by Ted Dexter about his action. It does look as if people from other countries refuse to believe that an Indian can

Karsan Ghavri in full swing.

bowl a good bouncer. Build is important but not everything. Malcolm Marshal is not as big-built as the rest of the West Indians are, but is still among the quickest in the world. Rhythm is equally important and Ramakant Desai had one of the most rhythmic run-ups ever in the history of the game. If one sat on a higher floor and watched Ramakant run in, one could see how every footprint was imprinted on the turf and how Ramakant would invariably run up with his steps falling on the exact place of the previous ball's run-up. For me who had seen Ramakant's first-class debut against the West Indies from the North stand at the Brabourne stadium, it was a special pleasure to play in his benefit game. When I came into the Bombay Ranji squad it was Ramakant, Ajit Wadekar and Babloo Gupte who made me feel comfortable. Sure, they pulled my leg but not sarcastically like a couple of other seniors did. In those days at lunch time there would be tables for four which used to be occupied by Ramakant, Ajit, Babloo and myself. The late Vijay Manjrekar was another person who was a tremendous help and though there is a great Bombay tradition of leg-pulling, it was done to make a newcomer feel comfortable and accepted. These senior and respected players did much to make us youngsters feel part of the team. The outstation tours by train were also a great experience where practically the whole team would gather in one cabin and listen to the cricketing experiences of the stalwarts. It was an unforgettable education. It is difficult to forget Hoshie Amroliwalla geeing Nari Contractor up to talk about the way he handled the West Indian fast bowlers. It was truly fascinating listening to these battle-hardened players, and it inspired one to try and emulate them. Unfortunately, today everyone travels by air and thus misses out on the togetherness that a train journey brings about.

Talking about air travel, some senior players in the Indian team did make efforts to get them upgraded from economy class but whether they succeeded, one does not know. It is a pity that such a rich cricket Board like ours should continue to send our team especially on such long air journeys by economy class. Not only would the executive class have been more comfortable but it would have given our players a little more privacy. From previous experience, one knows how team members who have been fast asleep have been suddenly woken up by a fellow passenger for an autograph. For shorter journeys, like to Sharjah, it is understandable if economy class tickets are purchased. Here also in the past certain players have paid the difference between the economy and first class themselves and travelled first class while the rest of the team has sat at the back. Wonder whether the Board is aware of that since it always worries about team spirit so much, and wonder also whether the Board officials when they travel for international meetings travel economy class.

The Board also did not go up in the cricketers' estimation by raising the tour fees by Rs 5000/- per player. This tight-fisted approach is hardly going to help the Board in its relations with the players because there seem to be different rules for the players and for the officials. After seeing the increase in foreign travel tax, the Board must be feeling quite happy that the team travelled to the West Indies before the tax came into force. Imagine another Rs 200/- per player would have set the Board back by Rs 3400/-. Not good for its financiers at all!

Anyways, all that is water under the bridge now as all eyes are focussed on our team's performance in West Indies. Nothing is impossible as Ajit Wadekar showed in 1971 and Kapil Dev in 1983. And if the team of 1989 does what Ajit's and Kapil's teams did, they are sure to travel first class on the way back! Good luck, guys!

02.03.1989

Right:
Manjrekar
team mate Sachin
early days; Raj
Dungarpur – the
...ntor.

YOUNG MANJREKAR
Shows the Way

When Sanjay Manjrekar played the stroke to get him his first Test century, he must have made plenty of people happy, none more than Raj Singh Dungarpur the much-maligned chairman of the selection committee. Not because Raj was one of the selectors who plumped for Sanjay but because Raj was a personal friend of the great Vijay and had seen Sanjay when he was a toddler. To see the baby grow up to become a man (and that is exactly what a century against the West Indies means) must have brought tears to Raj's eyes. Not only was he vindicated as a selector but it also exposed all those who criticised Sanjay's inclusion as ignoramuses.

Sanjay's class has been evident ever since he was a schoolboy but somehow he began to flower only during his university days and the century-hitting habit he has picked from there has continued, and one hopes, will continue. The danger of a century against the West Indies is that expectations are raised sky-high overnight and the people feel that a century is a must against lesser attacks. The other danger is that Sanjay may be asked to bat one-drop from the next Test if the tour selectors decide that Shastri and Sidhu should open and bring in Raman. Sanjay should be India's one-down batsman in due course but not now, for this is the time for him to establish himself in the side and he can do so batting lower down the order and getting more runs and confidence.

Azharuddin's injury is a big dampener. It is almost similar to the one that plagued Pakistan's Wasim Akram for the last couple of seasons. For a long time doctors believed it was a groin problem that kept recurring until they found recently that it was a stress fracture of the pelvic bone. Perhaps Azhar also should have another medical opinion because his problem is also becoming a chronic one. If Azhar is unfit for the third Test then Arun Lal may be able to keep his place and Raman or Ajay Sharma can come in for Azhar. Unfortunately, there is no first class game between the second and the third Test and there is thus no way of finding the form of these two players.

It is asking for too much perhaps but if Mohinder can be persuaded to play, it might just give the team the dose of experience that it is lacking at the moment. It would also take the pressure off Vengsarkar. Lack of practice has obviously hurt

Manjrekar in a pensive mood.

the Indian team and the weather is to blame but that, as Viv Richards would love to tell, is part of the game. However the captain is too good a batsman to fail and one big knock from him will not only help him with his captaincy but also be a big morale booster for his team. The home team captain is also due for a big score and since Jamaica is a ground where he has not yet scored a century (first-class or Test), he would be looking for one to set the record straight. If I have got the above information wrong, the statisticians could correct me and also inform the other cricketing buffs about the real position.

This is being written on the way to the West Indies so one does not know what has happened in the Barbados Test. Hopefully the rains will have come heavily and saved India, because then the West Indies will really feel the pressure as they are suspicious of the wicket at Trinidad. This wicket has always aided spin even if there is a thick layer of grass on it. The grass will make the bounce a little uneven which will be just the kind of help our bowlers need. But our batsmen need to give them a total to defend. Young Manjrekar has shown the way and if the others can follow his example then we would be in for an exciting match.

Just before I left, I was privileged to be asked to be on a three-member committee to suggest means to improve Bombay cricket. Obviously, the administrators at the Bombay Cricket Association (BCA) are worried about the fact that the Ranji is missing from their showcase for the past few years and have begun to take steps to try and correct that. For me, it will be an education to be able to sit with Polly Umrigar, and Ashok Mankad and discuss ways and means to improve Bombay's cricket with two of the shrewdest cricketing brains. But it is important to know that there are others who know Bombay cricket better than the members of the Bombay committee and the BCA, I am happy to say, is taking their advice and guidance. The various coaches, umpires and players like Shivalkar who are still playing local cricket will be able to give more inputs to the BCA. I even suggested that the press should be involved and the BCA should invite some of the sports writers to seek their views on how Bombay cricket can be improved. Hopefully, the BCA will do that so that all opinions and views are considered.

Here in London, the South African issue still looms large over the cricketing talk. The recent meeting of the cricketers' body in England pleaded with the Test and County Cricket Board (TCCB) to allow the cricketers to go and coach in South Africa or raise the minimum pay of the county's cricketers. Why this was being debated, Ian Botham, whose name does not figure in the shortlist announced by the English selectors, has dropped a big hint that he might consider going to South Africa if he is not picked this summer for England. The entire press corps has followed him to the Far East and Australia, just to see his comeback to cricket. Even if he is not a Test player, he is still a big media star as seen by the media following him round the world for his county's lung openers for the season. That is charisma. That is star power! That is Ian Botham.

13.04.1989

...Dev with that
...bowling action:
...Sharma, G.
...anath timing a shot.

VENGSARKAR Needed a Hand

Coming to America from the West Indies is an entirely different experience. From the laid-back placid way of life in the West Indies to the hustle and bustle of New York is a shock to the system. Even the colour of the sea is different, the different shades of dark blue, light blue and green of the Caribbean giving way to the dark grey sea as one flies over America. The colour of the sea and skyscrapers of Manhattan bring back memories of Bombay and it is no wonder that suddenly everybody is feeling homesick.

From the Indian point of view, the West Indies tour was an unmitigated disaster. The team was young and inexperienced and when up against a strong team like the West Indies, it was never going to be easy. With Viv Richards not having forgotten Madras, it was on the cards that they would go flat out to win every game, whether the One-dayers or Tests and that's what happened. Fortunately for the Indian team, only the wicket in the last Test was hard and bouncy and caused our batsmen great discomfort. One heard local commentators lambasting our batsmen for not getting behind the line of the ball but they were strangely silent whenever the West Indies pair was rooted onto their back-foot by a rejuvenated Kapil Dev and gutsy Chetan Sharma. In any case, from experience one learns that on a wicket like the one at Sabina Park, Kingston, it is better to play beside the ball rather than behind it. Gundappa Vishwanath would do that beautifully and thus a bouncy track never bothered him because by getting beside the ball, he was in a much better position to either leave it safely or score runs off it. Having seen our batsmen in the last Test gamely trying to battle away, one is confident that the same players with more experience behind them will encounter similar wickets on the next tour of the West Indies with greater ease than on this occasion.

Yet there is no doubting that the side missed experience. With Vengsarkar himself out of form, it was understandable that he was more worried about it and could not possibly give valuable tips to the younger players. It is easy to talk to juniors when one is doing well because one talks with the confidence and weight of performance behind one and Dilip could have done with another experienced hand to take the load off his shoulders. The manager being a bowler himself during his playing days was not in a position to give advice about batting and being a

Mohinder Amarnath cuts a ball to the boundary.

perfectionist meant that the players were constantly failling below his standards of expectations. They were thus apprehensive about approaching him and one heard from the members of the team that the man the players ran to for counsel was none other than Mohinder Amarnath who was in the West Indies as a media man.

The tour programme was also such that some members of the side barely got the chance to put on their flannels. Rain also was a spoilsport and this added to the lack of match practice for the team. The playing conditions specifying a minimum number of overs to be bowled in a day were also against the Indians. With their pacemen, the West Indies never bowled more than 10-12 overs an hour and with the sun setting early, they never really got down to bowling their full quota of overs for the day. This meant that the Indians faced less deliveries than the West Indies who got more deliveries to score off since the Indian attack was manned mainly by the spinners. This playing condition also meant that if the Indian innings terminated during the day with the West Indies far behind their quota, then the Indian bowlers had to make up and bowl the required number of overs.

So right from the programme of the tour to the selections and the playing conditions, the team was facing a tough battle. They lost their vice captain to an injury and there was nobody like Sandeep Patil, an Ashok Mankad, Eknath Solkar or even Maninder Singh to entertain the players with jokes and boost the drooping morale. If the West Indies tour was thus an unhappy one for some of the newcomers to the side, it was no surprise that some of them like Manjrekar who came out with their reputation enhanced was a bonus.

Off the field, the West Indies was the usual fun place. The variety in food and the music was terrific, as usual. One of the highlights of the tour was the dance organised by the West Indies Players Association to raise money for its coffers. The live music by famous Calypsonians had everybody tapping their feet and swaying their bodies as only the West Indies can. It was a pity that but for a few Indian players, nobody turned up. One would have thought that, since it was organised by the West Indian Players Association, every Indian player would turn up, since it was also on the eve of the rest day of the Test. But the Indians did not though the West Indies Players Association had promised some amount to the Indian Players Association. There were moves to revive the association towards the end of the tour but only time will tell if the feelings generated can be translated into action. On a long tour, it is easy to come together and talk about getting things done, but once one goes back home and to the regular routine, the assurances on the tour take a back seat. It was good to meet old friends in the West Indies like (Ispahani) Ali and the ebullient Alvin Thompson. Talking to them of the old times was a magical experience as one got transported to the past. But that was for just a fleeting moment or two, for the realities of today and the toll of age, and modern maladies, was right there in front of you. Charlie Davis who scored so heavily in 1971 is on limited time suffering from multiple sclerosis. The disease has not curbed his zest for life for he was there on all days of the Trinidad Test laughing the way he did in the past. The right eye does not close much now, the smile is a lot crooked and there is a very pronounced limp now. It was enough to teach one that there is a power above and to him everyone comes alike. There is a benefit game organised for him next season by Lance Gibbs and one hopes that it is success. Charlie Davis is comfortably off and perhaps could do without a benefit but it would be wonderful to be able to go and play and show him that however hard one plays on the field, there are plenty of players who care about each other off the field.

11.05.89

...d bottom,
...e Stadium
...the team
...celebrating the
...st Indies tour in

IT'S MY 100th

When the office told me that this is going to be my hundredth column I was pleasantly surprised. Time indeed has flown since the first column came out almost four years ago. Lots of things have happened in the sporting world, some exciting, some dull, and some controversial ones. One has tried to write about those moments in as balanced a view as is humanly possible. Of course there is no such thing as the perfect column just as there is no such thing as a perfect cricketer. Everybody who writes tries to get there, most of us fall way below the standard, some, very few, get close to the perfect column and that is when reading becomes a pleasure. Unfortunately, those pleasures have been far and few between. And one never gives up looking for something interesting to read.

The first time I wrote was way back in the early 1970s. If I remember rightly then it was an article in *Sportsweek* about the future of Indian cricket. It was not a serious piece but a tongue-in-cheek one because it was also written about the sons of my cricketing colleagues and how they would take over in the last decade of the century. As if sons of cricketers automatically take up to cricket. Most in fact take up some other sport or another career away from sport. History is replete with examples of sons who have fallen by the wayside in trying to follow in the footsteps of their fathers in international cricket. The biggest disadvantage they face is their father's reputation. The old timers who have seen the father will never ever agree that the son is better though he actually may be so.

Since that article got a fairly good response from the readers, it encouraged me to keep on writing. With the Cricket Control Board's contract it was difficult to write regularly. Till 1977, the contracts were so tight and binding that it was a hard job to breathe but like any youngster one just wanted to play cricket then and nothing else mattered. However, in 1976, on the West Indian tour, the Cricketer's Association (not Players Association, please note) was formed. And that changed the scene. The cricketers were united as never before although various pressures were brought on individuals to break away from the Association and most importantly, they had faith in the leaders of the Association. To be sure the leaders were the top players of that time and in spite of what ignorant and biased people may say, players who were solely interested in the welfare of the Indian cricketer and Indian cricket. Those were the years when Indian cricket was at the top. Those were the years that the cricketing world was torn asunder by the World Cricket Series. Those were also the years when the officials of the Board were interested in the welfare of Indian cricket and not in their power play. No wonder Indian cricket flourished during that period as the players had no other tensions or pressures.

Somewhere in the early 1980s, things began to change in the Indian Cricket Board and power politics crept in. The ouster of Mr. Wankhede as the president of the Board in spite of having one year to go was the first sign of this. Suddenly, all the officials began to watch their backs so as not to be stabbed as poor Mr. Wankhede was and in watching their backs they lost sight of the future of Indian Cricket. We won a couple of One-day championships but our performances, by and large, were either average or below average. Most unluckily, the players who were as solid as rocks were dragged unwittingly into the vortex of power politics and thus broken by fuelling their personal cricketing ambitions. Hopefully, this is just a cycle and the wheel will turn for a new phase where cricket will be played and administered by people who only have Indian cricketers', interest at heart and nothing else.

The media also has had enormous changes. On the 1971 tour of West Indies, which was my first tour, I remember there were only three or four Indian journalists who were covering the tour. There was neither TV nor any radio commentary. Thus the only way reports of the match were conveyed to cricket lovers was through the newspapers. Since there were only three or four journalists, they became part of the team that everyone got on well with each other. Yes, there was criticism if the performance was bad but it was never criticism with the intention of 'getting' the player nor were any motives implied when a player failed to perform to his potential. There was a realisation that there is another team playing as well and thus having its own strategy and tactics to prevent the success of our players. Too often today this realisation seems to be missing as players are 'got at' and motives imagined and implied for their performances. This could be the result of a mushrooming of the media. There is today satellite communication which enables us to see the action within hours of the event if not live and thus the pressure on the player has increased as they are now subjected to scrutiny of more than three or four pairs of eyes. The sports lovers who thus get to see most of the action on their TV screens in their living rooms now want a little more than just a report of the same. They want an analysis of the performances and the whys and the why nots and thus who have played the game before coming into the frame as writers. They do not necessarily write better than the professional writers just as professional cricketers do not play better than the regular players. Yet the reading public wants to know about it from the former players' pen. That's also because there are no more Carduses, no more Eingletons, no more Ray Robinsons. Yes, there are plenty of knowledgeable and talented writers but somehow falling short of the standard set by the above-mentioned gentlemen. Or it could simply be that this columnist is an old-timer who feels that the 'sons' aren't as good as the 'fathers'!

Thank you dear readers, for bearing with me for so long. As in any 'Century' there are some good shots, some bad ones, some playing and missing and some edging. I do hope I've given you more of the first than the others.

17.08.1989

... Bordi ... the ... (opposite right) ... al Gavas- ... a pak conference; ... ngton, during ... ng days.

MANAGERS... Those Vital Men

Watching the easy informality between Chandu Borde and the Indian team brought to the fore the importance of a good manager. In fact the appointment of the manager of the Indian cricket team is as important as the selection. The man chosen for the job must have an instant rapport with the team for on a tour there is simply no time to build up one. And a rapport can be instant when the players not only have admiration for the past deeds of the manager but also respect for the man for his temperament and for the fairness in his attitude towards all the players. Then, even if there are players in the side who have a better playing record than the manager, there is seldom any trouble. Above all, if the manager has a sense of humour then he will be able to not only take the odd bit of leg pulling in the proper spirit but perhaps give back as good as he got.

The first manager I toured under was Keki Tarapore. After the 1971 team to the West Indies was declared, we were asked to assemble for nets at the Brabourne Stadium. As we were practising, suddenly we saw a man with a spring-heeled walk and one sleeve rolled high up come to the ground. It was Keki and he went around introducing himself to the rest of the team but his manner suggested that he knew he was our boss and we better remember it. There is no doubt that he cared for his team but he was not willing to show it lest the players take advantage of that and so he did not smile too much excepting when Dilip Sardesai was up to his usual pranks. We had some big names on that tour, Wadekar the captain, Jaisimha, Bedi, Prasanna, Durani, Abid Ali and Sardesai. And what great seniors they were. Practically, every evening we all would gather in one room and talked cricket till it was time to sleep. Listening to them was an experience as well as an inspiration. While Keki did not join these gatherings, he would pop by once in a while ostensibly to have a word with Ajit but perhaps more to make sure that none of us youngsters were indulging ourselves with a drop or two. He needn't have worried for excepting the first meeting where we were repeatedly asked whether we were sure we did not want a drink, there was never an attempt made to force us to have one which later on another skipper would do. Though Keki's demeanour was forbidding, there was no doubt that he was fond of his team and especially the

Chandu Borde with Sachin Tendulkar.

younger ones who did not want to be led astray. Here was an example of a man who had played only one Test but was able to control a team because of his personality.

There have been other managers of the Indian team and all have had varying effects on the side. The best non-cricketing manager has been Fatehsinghrao Gaekwad. By non-cricketing, I mean one who has not played in international cricket. On our first tour of Pakistan in 1978, Fatehsinghrao was an immense success with not just the team but with the people of Pakistan. At airports, there would be huge crowds to welcome him and the crowds would move with him after garlanding him profusely, leaving us cricketers stranded on the tarmac to fend for ourselves. He did a truly magnificent job on a difficult tour when there were plenty of flashpoints. Yes, we had a good deputy in 'Peter' Man Singh who went on to manage the victorious World Cup side in 1983. Yet there was no mistaking who was the real star of the Indian team in Pakistan in 1978.

The Pakistani team has had Intikhab Alam as manager for some time now and 'Inti' has done a great job from all accounts. If the Indian team has 'ego' problems then the Pakistani team has some more. But 'Inti' has been able to keep all of them in firm control. Here again is the classic example of a person who has achieved some eminence in Test cricket and also is known for his sense of fairplay and humour. No wonder players respond to him.

Bobby Simpson is another example of a former player who has done a remarkable job as a manager. When he became the cricket manager, he said his aim was to do such a good job that there would never be a need for a manager for cricket. The way Australians have played in the past couple of seasons and particularly in England in the Ashes series is a tribute to Bobby Simpson's planning and foresight. He was there to spot the flaws in the English team and think up means to take advantage of them. The results are very well known. It was he who insisted on a left hander-right hander combination for opening the batting. In doing so, he broke up the successful opening partnership of Boon-Marsh. Once again the success of the Taylor-Marsh combine is adequate proof of how thorough Simpson's reading of the game was.

Mickey Stewart of England has not been as successful but then the pressures on England players from its media are unique and this perhaps is a major reason why they are floundering at the moment. However, most other times where a manager has struck a rapport quickly with his team, though the tour may not be successful, it certainly has been an enjoyable one.

Today, Chandu Borde's rapport with his team can be easily seen. He has to make use of this rapport to steer the team in the right direction for one fears that there are moves to look at things other than cricket. To get his players to think only about cricket and nothing else should be Borde's aim and if he succeeds even fifty percent in doing that, then the performance of the team will be well worth watching. Else the spectators and cricket lovers will say 'So what's new?'

14.10.1989

*...ise:
...Azad; Kapil with
...Ravi Shastri and
...ndian legend –
...Richards.*

THEY ALL MADE
Ekki's Smile Wider

First things first, and so a big thank you to all those who turned up at the Wankhede stadium to honour Eknath Solkar. Also, to the sponsors ITC, the BCA and the local sponsors who helped to make this benefit match a success. Mention must also be made of B. Arun Kumar & Co. who very generously bought a section of Vijay Merchant stand tickets as well as those two indefatigable cricket lovers Prakash Palekar and Prakash Kelkar, who slogged to make sure that everything was hitch free. Eknath was his usual self, cheerful and happy to see the crowd enjoy themselves.

The match itself had its spectacular moments, especially when Kirti Azad and Bhaskar Pillai were batting for Delhi. There were some great strokes played by the duo during their partnership. The two sixers that Kirti hit were truly memorable. In fact, Kirti loves to hit the ball out of the Wankhede stadium everytime he plays in Bombay. Bhaskar Pillai scored a delightful century, but even that was not enough for him to get into the Indian team. What Bhaskar should do is to change his birth certificate and show his age as twenty and also begin to bowl a bit of spin so he will then be picked as a youngster and also as a spinner who can bat a bit.

After all, whether he spins the ball or is likely to take wickets does not matter. The last few spinners capped have not taken many wickets but have shown pleasing stubbornness with the bat. And that Bhaskar will do very well.

Speaking of caps, it is about time our Board differentiated between an India cap for One-day internationals and for Tests. England and Australia have separate caps and separate sweaters and blazers for One-day players and Test players. Test matches are the real thing, and every player's ultimate aim should be to win the India Test cap. Mind you, on tour abroad where the programme includes both Tests and One-day internationals, then the India Test caps should be given but when the team plays One-dayers at home or in a One-day tourney like Sharjah then separate One-day caps should be given.

The decision not to take an injured Wassan, to Sharjah needs to be lauded but, how can a batsman replace a bowler? Have the people who matter forgotten that our One-day World Cup wins have been when we have dismissed the opposition. As it is one of our more successful bowlers especially in Sharjah, Narendra Hirwani has been dropped on the grounds that he cannot bat but in a side where Kiran More is likely to bat number nine, do we need Hirwani's batting? Or do we need his wicket taking abilities? Haven't we seen over the years that the bits and pieces Indian cricketer goes to pieces in international cricket. The only genuine all-rounders India has had in the past decade are Kapil Dev and Ravi Shastri. They complemented each other very well for Shastri was more accomplished as a batsman and Kapil as a bowler and both would have made the Indian team on their one talent alone. The other all-rounder in recent times is Manoj Prabhakar who has come up so well in the last season. If only Manoj could direct his aggression solely at the opposition rather than the umpire, he and his side will benefit greatly.

Pressure can make people react in different ways and we have seen how the topmost players in the world react in an uncharacteristic manner. The normally unflappable and ever smiling Des Haynes showed a different side of his personality when saddled with the pressure of captaincy though of course it is perfectly possible that the British media may have overplayed the exchange 'Dezzy' had with Alec Stewart. One must not forget that in the eyes of the British media, the tabloids in particular, most English cricketers on tour are saints who never cheat, never

pressurise umpires, never sledge, never bend the rules and such other activities which only the opposition does. And if the umpire gives a wrong decision favouring the home team then it is biased umpiring but of course if an English umpire gives a similar wrong decision then it is an error of judgement.

No wonder Viv Richards got incensed with the reporting and confronted the reports of a tabloid writer for the piece he had written. Viv should have done it after the game or much before the day's play began but by not leading the team on the field he did not help the team's cause, for his players must have been aware why he was missing and part of their minds would have been to see the result of Viv's confrontation with the journalist.

Ravi Shastri

Viv has come out the poorer for the episode and there is a lesson in it for his Glamorgan colleague Ravi Shastri. Viv's troubles started with his reaction to the section of the crowd comprising British tourists to Antigua. Everybody will say that a player's job is simply to play and not to respond to the baiting of the crowd but nobody will say that the crowd's job is to simply watch the game. When one buys tickets for a game, the price does not include freedom to abuse players or throw things at them. Sure there is going to be disappointment or even disenchantment with some player's performances but if the reaction to the superb performance is prolonged applause then the reaction to a bad performance should be absolute silence. Why throw rubbish at a player when he does badly when one does not throw valuables at him when he does well? But then crowds will be crowds and a player with a sound temperament will not get carried away by applause nor get worked up with criticism. A simple gesture can often get a hostile crowd on one's side while an angry response will invite not just the hostile section but most of the crowd to go against you. What Ravi Shastri needs is to get that gesture right and he will find that those who he feels are against him are not really against him but going along with what has become a fad. Some fads stay on and some fade away and Ravi would do well to remember that!

25.04.90

wise:
mmad
addin;
Gavaskar, and
Channel 9 cricket
entator Richie
d.

Learning From the **GREAT BENAUD**

What an education and experience it has been commentating for the BBC. It is totally different from anything else that I have experienced in my nascent stages of TV commentating. I have never done any commentary for Doordarshan, so it is difficult to know whether they employ the same methods now, but having been in their box for some interviews on occasions I do know that they were not in existence then.

Here at the BBC the producer is constantly in touch with the commentator and summariser via the headphones, and the commentators and summarisers too are in touch with the producers in the OB van with the console they have in front of them. Thus, if there is concentration of the camera on a player, the producer instructs you via the headphones to speak about him. Similarly, if the commentator or the summariser wishes to speak about a particular incident or player, then they can through the consoles in front of them speak asking the producer to keep the cameras on a player or the video recording action replay ready. The commentator can also ask for a particular statistical record to be shown which is then flashed on to the screen for the commentator/summariser to remark about.

This aspect of being constantly in touch with the producer who sits in the OB van with the controls that show the picture on the screen is the aspect which I feel is different from anywhere else that I have given commentary from.

My first day at Leeds for the first One-dayer was a nervous one and particularly as my first stint was with as experienced a commentator as Richie Benaud who has been at it for over twenty-five years. Richie can be poker-faced most of the time and this trait of his can really be intimidating when you might say something light-hearted and expect him to crack a smile, and he does not.

But any feeling of intimidation and nervousness disappeared when, before the Trentbridge One-dayer, Richie took me aside and said, 'If I may make a small suggestion' and then went on to give me some great advice particularly with the way to hold the microphone. In the Leeds One-dayer, I kept holding the mike a few inches from my lips all the time. This meant that my fellow commentators did not know whether I wanted to speak or not. Richie's advice was to keep the mike (which is incidentally with the lead) on my thigh because then my fellow commentator would know I did not have any comment to make and if he asked me a question which I wanted to reply, it would give me that precious second or two to gather my thoughts and answer.

By the way, there are three commentators, Richie Benaud, Jack Bannister and Tony Lewis and there summarisers—Ray Illingworth, Geoff Boycott and myself. All three commentators

With Geoff Boycott, enjoying a lighter moment.

have their own mike sponges which they put on when it is their turn at the mike and 'Illy' and 'Geoff' have their own headphones to tune in to the producer. The newcomer uses the equipment handed over by BBC.

In the morning before the game starts and sometimes just during lunch and tea intervals, we have to do an invision piece with Tony Lewis or Richie Benaud where the wickets fallen are discussed or any other cricketing subject. When Gooch was playing his marathon innings, Boycott and I were asked about opening the batting and its problems and advantages.

Geoffrey Boycott is absolutely brilliant as a summariser. His technical expertise at the crease was legendary but the way he explains the same on TV is an education by itself to any youngster tuning in. He is clear, precise and his vocabulary was surprisingly good. He also made a few bloomers liking 'looking back in hindsight', etc. But then all these bloomers are put up on a board next to where the commentators sit and they are looked back on with great amusement at the end of the day and then every morning. It certainly has been enjoyable so far, and an education and a good experience as I said at the beginning of the piece.

Lack of experience is really what cost India the first Test. Captain Azharuddin in his fourth Test as skipper asked England to bat after winning the toss which really meant India was on the backfoot from that moment. Perhaps with Kapil at his best that decision would have made more sense but Kapil's bowling is not the same, and though Manoj passed the bat often before lunch on the first day, there was no more than one wicket that India could show for their skipper's decision, when nothing short of four wickets would have justified it. However, the point to be remembered is that the decision was taken not for any selfish reason but with the team's interest at heart and thus ought not to have been condemned the way it was by the cricket manager. But when it comes to saving one's skin the manager is very quick to put the blame on the players. Remember 'the Pacific Ocean and committing suicide' statements. They were all meant to shift the blame elsewhere. The point is that if as a cricket manager a little responsibility and thinking is not going to be inculcated in the team then he is not good enough. Enough has been said in my earlier reports from England so I will not touch upon it here except to say that the reason for the Indian team's performances after their fine showing in Pakistan is that they are playing 'brainless cricket'.

Once more I am off, leading an old world XI in an exhibition game in Toronto between the first and second Test match. The World team has got two other Indians, Vishy and Engineer, and three Pakistanis, Mushtaq, Inkhitab and Haroon Rashid. The two new-ball bowlers will be Graham McKenzie and Bob Massie and the opener will be Glen Turner. Duleep Mendis is also in the side, so it does look like we have a fair batting line up. Problem is that the old West Indies team have more than a fair opening pair bowlers in Andy Roberts and Michael Holding. For spin, they have those two pals of mine, Ramadhin and Valentine. The batting will be led by Hunte and Nurse with Kanhai (Skipper), Gomes and the one and only Gary Sobers to follow. It should be interesting and one only hopes that the outfield is fast, so no one will have to do any chasing of the strokes hit by either side's batsmen.

The story about my declining the invitation to be a member of the MCC broke here during the Test match though one had done so almost eight months back. I do not understand the fuss created, for I had my reasons and besides one cannot accept life membership of every club that writes to one. What was surprising was the reaction of the Press Box, where practically every English scribe congratulated me for 'showing the "Gestapo" its place'. The photographers here too came and pumped my hand in appreciation. So when our cricket manager sent his open letter to me just a few minutes ago, they were incredulous. Their reaction to the cricket manager's letter is not publishable and my reaction was no reaction since the letter was not even worthy of an instant comment. All I can remind the cricket manager is that I rejected the invitation to be a member of the MCC while he was rejected by the MCC.

02.08.1990

Right,
Sulnman Bukhatir
was playing a shot

WHAT KAPIL DEV Needs...

Since this column appears in most of the publications on a Sunday and in others just before or after the Sunday, let me start by wishing Kapil Dev many happy returns (6 January) and a very Happy Birthday. Also from the Indian cricketing point of view one would like to wish him a return to the days when he regularly demolished the top half of the opposition India was playing.

Many theories have been worked out to tell the world why Kapil's strike rate has declined. While most attribute it to too mush cricket and some experts like Ray Illingworth (the best international captain I have known) feel that there is some minor technical problem. Kapil himself has hinted in a recent interview that too much of One-day cricket may have contributed to his decline. Kapil explained that in One-day cricket one has to bowl the incoming ball more than the outgoing ball and so he has to a certain extent lost control over the outswinger which was his deadliest delivery.

All these factors may have contributed, but the most important reason I feel, is that Kapil has nobody to compete with, within the Indian team. When he broke into the Indian team, there were other bowlers who were more famous than he was and there were batsmen in the team who were a challenge to his bowling. In the nets he would let out a joyous shout every time he got a batsman out or playing a false stroke. There were some batsmen like Dilip Vengsarkar and Yashpal Sharma to whom he bowled with the same hostility as in a match. The net practice was thus very productive and helped to improve not just his bowling but also his attitude to the batsmen. Out in the middle, the Pakistanis tried to unnerve him by using the choicest of Punjabi words but all it did was to toughen him up and learn that Test cricket is no picnic. Having come from Chandigarh, he had the burning desire to prove himself the equal if not a better cricketer than the other big town boys and it was this burning desire to prove himself that I as a captain fuelled continuously. And what marvellous results we got. For example, if I found that 'Kaps' was flagging off a bit towards the end of the fourth over without a wicket, I would run up from my position in the slips to him in the middle of the over as he walked back to his bowling mark and he would look at me as if I had instructions for him. All I would say is that 'I have come to give you a little breather while I

With Kapil Dev, sharing a lighter moment.

walk back slowly to slips.' Without fail the next three overs would be the quickest he would bowl just to prove to me that he was not tired and needed no breathers. The other bait which provoked a similar response would be to ask him if it was alright if 'Kiri' stood up to the stumps. Of course, having finished that query, all of us behind the wicket including Kiri would step back a few paces for the next few overs as the ball would thud into Kiri's gloves.

Similarly, in batting, he would make batting look the easiest thing in the world and get thirty odd in no time and then in response to the crowd's demand for a six would lose his wicket hitting a catch in the deep. So, I said in a magazine article that Kaps would not score a fifty again. Lo and behold, the match after the article appeared, he scored a most brilliant half-century I have seen on one of the nastiest wickets. He came back to the pavilion and said, 'Skip, I got a fifty'. He had a point to prove.

Today he has nothing to prove to anybody and being the seniormost in the team, has no one to combat with for being the star of the show. What he needs is someone in the team to be a challenge to him, to provoke him, to rile him, to needle him, to cajole him, to ignore him and then finally to thump him on the back in appreciation of his efforts. That is why when last month at the function to release the video cassettes of his company, he said to me quietly, 'I miss you in the team, sunshine'; it was the greatest compliment that I will receive from a fellow cricketer. May your birthday be a happy one Kaps. May you return to the high wicket-taking standards that you have set for yourself.

The cancellation of the short tour by the West Indies and the consequent rescheduling of the Wills, Deodhar and Zonal Ranji matches have upset the plans of the beneficiaries who had opted for a Ranji game as their benefit. Since a benefit is once in a lifetime thing, care should be taken to see that wholesale rescheduling of games does not take place at the last moment leaving the beneficiary in the lurch. All his plans can just go to waste if some of the top players have to play somewhere else. In fact, if a Ranji game is a benefit, then it should be so rescheduled that the beneficiary derives the maximum benefit out of it. The recent Bombay-Baroda game which was a benefit for J.J. Kore is an example. Originally the game was to be in Thane which would have ensured a good purse for the beneficiary, but once the dates were changed the ground at Thane was unavailable and the new venue Wankhede stadium did nothing but add to the beneficiary's woes.

Two other beneficiaries who lost out were the Indian players who would have been honoured by the CBFS in Sharjah. The Indian Board's stubborn refusal to go to Sharjah, in spite of the West Indies tour being cancelled deprived the players of a benefit. Yet the show at Sharjah went ahead with only Pakistan and Sri Lanka participating. Abdul Rehman Bukhatir deserves to be complimented for sticking to his guns in spite of knowing that it would be a loss-making tourney. The CBFS also gave two Pakistani cricketers a benefit and showed administrators round the world that irrespective of whether they make profits or losses, their commitment to the cricketers remain and truly live up to their name—Cricketers Benefit Fund Series. May they go from strength to strength every year and you dear readers, have a wonderful, memorable happy sporting year!

01.01.1991

...vise:
...West Indian greats
...arfield Sobers,
...Greenidge, Sir
...Richards and
...d Haynes.

WHY I AM OFF to South Africa

After my last column was submitted and despatched, arrived the much discussed invitation from South Africa to attend the banquet to celebrate · the unification of the two factions of South African cricket into one multiracial United Cricket Board of South Africa. It was too late to change the column though perhaps the Bombay papers could have carried it but it certainly would not have been fair to the outstation papers and so we let the column be as it was.

The government was very quick to clear my trip and I should be leaving soon to attend the banquet. Over the last few days, I have been asked by lots of people what I hope to achieve by my visit. The answer is nothing. I am not going there to achieve anything. I am simply an invitee to a banquet. I have no *locus standi* other than that for me to achieve anything by my visit. However, in the short time I am there, I will certainly keep my eyes and ears open. Not having been there before, please don't expect me to notice any changes for only people who live there would be qualified to talk about the changes that have taken place over the years. I would be happy simply to be in the company of the greatest cricketer the world has known, Sir Garfield Sobers, and if possible, to renew acquaintances with my Rest of the World teammates of 1971, the Pollock brothers and Hylton Ackerman. By the way, those with long memories might recall that soon after that tour of Australia, I was spelling my first name with a Y instead of an I and that was the influence of Ackerman, my opening partner who spelt his first name similarly. Fortunately I got back to my original spelling soon enough before the sniping could begin.

The sniping has begun though for Viv Richards and his team. After their defeats in the One-dayers, the cricketing world expected them to bounce back, literally, in the Test matches but they have lost the first Test quite comprehensively and it will require real character for them to come back. To be sure they have done so in the past but then time does take its toll and the razor-sharp keenness is not quite there either in their batting or in their bowling. The absence of Gordon Greenidge is a big blow especially as Desmond Haynes is not fully fit. Haynes' back problem is fairly old and its recurrence in what is a cold wet summer means that he will always be weighed down with the worry of aggravating it and thus

Sir Vivian Richards – the class act.

will not be his free flowing self. Phillip Simmons is a mindless slogger who gives a bad name to the opening batting profession. Unless it's his lucky day it is hard to see him being a success in that position. Brian Lara is certainly a better prospect than Simmons and has shown that he has the temperament to match his skill in the limited opportunities that he has received. If Hooper could be promoted to open the batting and he has the technique to succeed, then Lara could be fitted into the eleven. As it is, Hooper has been struggling to score runs and perhaps the additional responsibility might just be the tonic he needs to convert his undoubted ability into runs for his side.

Most importantly, Viv Richards has to lead from the front and that means promoting himself to number four in the order. It was alright for him to bat lower when the West Indies were winning but now that they are struggling he has to show the way, particularly since he has expressed the desire to quit on an unbeaten note. Observing him bat over the last couple of years, one has noticed a change in his grip which opens the face of the bat far more than before. Now his bat seems to rest only on the inside bottom edge rather than the complete bottom as in his hey day when the bat face was also not easily visible to the bowler. He thus keeps slicing his drives and often gets outside edges to his favourite flicks to leg. Another noticeable difference in his batting is that he is not as quickly onto his front foot as before. It was very rare to see Viv Richards out leg-before, defending on the back foot but he has been dismissed in the One-dayers like that and it shows that he is not in form and knows it and thus is tentative on the front foot. At this level, it is just a matter of one good long century innings for everything to start clicking again but it's been two years since he has scored a Test century, though for all you know this being written on the eve of the second Test, he may well be batting with one under his belt by the time this is printed. And don't forget Lord's is his favourite ground.

The West Indian bowling machine continues to be as mean as ever though since all of them play county cricket, they may not be as frightening to the English batsmen as to the others. The problem is that in their extra efforts for pace, they end up over-stepping which swells the opposition score. While this is unforgivable in One-day cricket, it can be costly even in a closely fought Test match and with the West Indian batting looking a little brittle, every run is vital. If the West Indian fast bowlers can discipline themselves as far as no-balls and wides are concerned, then they will go a long way in helping West Indies come back to the top. There are still four Tests to go and three of them are likely to be played on flat wickets. Lord's, excepting for the first day, is now a batting wicket, Birmingham has always been a beautiful batting track and Oval though bouncy, thanks to the presence of Waqar Younis in the Surrey side is also favourable to the batsman who is patient. The West Indian fast bowlers will thus have to work hard for the wickets and if the sun comes out then their tasks will become a lot more difficult. The Lord's Test thus becomes crucial. The West Indies have to win it to avoid the pressure building up. Champions are known to delve deep into their reserves and come up with something extra. We shall soon see if the West Indians have that to keep their title as the Champions of Cricket!

19.06.1991

ALI, SOUTH AFRICA'S
Bread and Bacher!

There must already be quite a few words written about our South Africa trip as there were three journalists from India covering the visit for their newspapers. Not having read their dispatches, I do not know what their impressions were of a country of which there is very little idea in ours. Of course, Johannesburg is not South Africa but it is the commercial capital of the country and so important in its own way. There is great similarity to Australia, and Johannesburg is like a bigger Melbourne. If Johannesburg is like Melbourne then Soweto with its slums is like certain areas of Bombay, including a big ground which reminds one of the Azad Maidan. The slums are called squatters in South Africa.

It was here in Soweto that one saw a potential fast bowler for South Africa. He was about Malcolm Marshall's height with a smooth run-up and a nice action. Sir Garfield was much impressed with the lad, though when he was introduced to the great man and asked whether he had heard of Sobers, the youngster replied in the negative saying he had heard of Wes Hall. When the story reaches Barbados, there will be much mirth, and the current Minister of Tourism in the Barbados Government, Wes Hall himself is going to dine out a few times with this story. Wes and Sir Garfield are good friends and Sir Garfield is presently promoting tourism for Barbados.

By the time this is published, there will be indications whether South Africa will be readmitted into the International Cricket Conference. Although Sir Garfield's visit was approved by the Barabados government, there is doubt whether the other governments in the West Indies will support the case for readmission. By refusing permission to Imran Khan to attend the banquet, Pakistani government has already tipped its hand and as far as India is concerned, the External Affairs Ministry spokesman has made it clear when permission was given to me to visit South Africa that it does not indicate a change in policy of the government towards South Africa.

Speaking to Dr. Ali Bacher, one got the impression that he was confident that India would propose South Africa's readmission. How he got that impression is clear to those of us who were in South Africa and if it was only a case of pulling wool over his eyes then it is really not fair, for he has really worked hard for racial integration in

Dr. Ali Bacher, the perfect administrator.

sport in South Africa. To the coloured people in South Africa, the same Bacher means much more than Sobers and he is looked upon as a godfather there and I use the word in the nicest possible sense. Unfortunately, just before the unification meeting, Dr. Bacher's mother, who had been unwell for sometime, became critically ill and my last glimpse of Dr. Bacher was him forlornly making his way out of Johannesburg airport where he had come to see us off after receiving a call to go to the hospital immediately. There has been no news about his mother since, but hopefully when he arrives in London in a couple of days, he will be able to tell me that his mother is on the road to recovery. He deserves that for he is truly a fine human being who really cares for his countrymen irrespective of colour and creed.

The meeting held to officially unite the two boards was brief and businesslike with the media and special guests present alongwith the representatives of the various State Cricket Organizations. While observing these proceedings, the thought did cross my mind that while I was attending a meeting of the United Cricket Board of South Africa, I have not yet attended a meeting of our Cricket Board and am unlikely to do so in the future as well.

The banquet to celebrate the unification was a grand affair with over 700 people attending it. Since it was not a stag dinner there was plenty of colour which made it even more dazzling than ever. There were some good speeches by E.W. Swanton and Krish Makherduj, the vice-president of the new Board. Sir Garfield Sobers and Richie Benaud started well but got flatter as they went on. It was a long session with the whole banquet taking almost five hours and thus many an invitee was found to be slumping with his head on his shoulders due to too much good wine and too long speeches. Yet, it was a historic occasion and in a sense South Africa has taken a major step. Whether that step leads in the right direction is what the rest of the cricketing world will watch with great interest, I am sure.

While all this was memorable stuff because it was my first visit to the country, the most memorable event was the meeting with Dr. Nelson Mandela. I had missed the meeting which was hastily arranged for Sir Garfield immediately after the unification of the two Boards meeting in the morning. I left soon after this unification meeting to visit an Indian Centre and thus was not around when Sir Garfield Sobers' meeting with Dr. Mandela was fixed. Another meeting was thus arranged for me early next morning as Dr. Mandela was to fly to Durban for the first meeting of the A.N.C. in thirty years inside South Africa. And what a truly memorable meeting it was.

Even as I was saying 'it was an honour and privilege to meet you Sir,' he was responding with 'it is an honor to meet you and thank you for finding time to visit us'. It was unbelievable. Here was the great man thanking me for finding the time when it was quite simply the other way around. The humility he displayed, his clear thinking and alertness of mind and the lack of bitterness in spite of his imprisonment for twenty nine years is an example to us all. Here truly is a giant of a man who plays with a straight bat all the time. May his tribe increase, especially in the troubled times we live today.

04.06.1991

YORKSHIRE STINT
Will Toughen Sachin

The 'new Yorkshireman's' early innings have not quite lifted the clouds that have hovered over Yorkshire cricket for the past few years. The build up to his being not only the first overseas but also the first non-Yorkshire born cricketer has been so great that everyone expected him to be a success straightaway. However, the game of cricket can sometimes be cruel and expectations can die a quick death. In Sachin's case, of course, there is a long season ahead and he has plenty of opportunities to show his rare skills. Already, with his ever smiling face, he has managed to change slightly the dour Yorkshire image and may be before the season ends, all the Yorkshire players will be sporting smiles like our little sensation.

There is no question in my mind that the stint with Yorkshire will do him good. Yorkshire is a place where cricket has been a religion for years and Yorkshiremen do not praise others easily. The fact that Sachin has been asked to play for them itself is a great compliment. It will toughen him up mentally and his sheer enthusiasm for the game will mean that he will not mind the grind of cricket, day in, and day out. Fortunately, he will have friends who will be driving his car from city to city so that he can rest adequately between matches. Technically, too, he will benefit by learning how to play the moving ball as also to be a little patient with restrictive bowling. He is predominantly a front-foot player, so there again, there will be no big adjustment required to be made. If the fear is that the bouncier pitches in South Africa will trouble him after a season of coming on to the front foot, then one should look at the way he scored runs in Australia in spite of being a front-foot player. Most importantly, he is going at the right age where he can soak in so much about cricket by playing in the circuit which has got some great players. Others who go when they are established Test players might not enjoy the experience, for their technique and temperament is well set, but at Sachin's age there is always room for improvement and modification for the better. Also, so far he has been cocooned by his well-wishers and close friends and the Indian team which is also fiercely protective of him, so playing where he is away from them will also help him to be more self-reliant and independent. It is an education in more senses than one and knowing his temperament, one is confident that he will come through the experience a better person. I am very optimistic and I don't think that he has to be a great success on the field for his stint to be considered a success, for I am concerned with the overall experience which will benefit him and in turn, Indian cricket. So I don't believe his accepting the Yorkshire invitation to be a mistake as some others who themselves played several seasons of county cricket and did not think then that that was a mistake. But then one must concede that these critics are consistent with their double standards. What they do is okay, but if someone else does the same thing, it is not okay. Fortunately, Sachin is aware that their credibility is so poor that even their reflections in the mirror do not believe a word of what they are blabbering.

Equally fortunately, Sachin is not in the running for the Indian captaincy or else vested interests would have found fault with his batting grip and said that he is not fit for captaincy. As I had predicted in an earlier column, the captaincy issue will keep simmering for a while and come to a boil just as the new Indian season begins. Anywhere a current or former cricketer goes, he is asked for his views on the Indian captaincy. The latest is M.L. Jaisimha who has opined that Azhar should not be blamed for the team's performances and its losses. His buddy Mansur Ali Khan Pataudi has finally come out into the open and said that Kapil Dev should be reappointed as captain. In the editorial which he wrote for his sports weekly, Pataudi had commented in response to my suggestion that Kapil Dev be made player-manager of the Indian team that it would be an excellent idea if you did not wish him to get any more wickets or runs. Typically, Pataudi did not elaborate why he thought that as player-manager Kapil Dev would not make more runs or take more wickets. One has to presume, therefore, that he thought the responsibility of the job would impair Kapil's effectiveness as a cricketer. With his suggestion now that Kapil should be made captain, Pataudi is perhaps implying that the captaincy has little or no responsibility. That is hard to understand because just as the manager has to think about his players, so does the captain, and while a manager's responsibility ends off the field, the captain's not only begins on the field but is also extended off the field in discussions on strategy and tactics. Of course, captaincy during Pataudi's time and today is vastly different, with the Indian cricket lovers and the media being definitely less tolerant with failure now than before. While Pataudi thought that my suggestion was possibly made tongue-in-cheek, there is no doubt that the vast majority of cricket lovers know that Pataudi is employed by one of Kapil Dev's companies (Pataudi's words not mine). They are also aware that Pataudi was the one who interviewed Manoj Prabhakar and got him to say that either Shastri or Kapil should be made captain. Now even a kid who has just started taking interest in the game will tell you that in the aftermath of the World Cup, Shastri has as much chance of being the captain in October as the sun of rising in the West. Yet Pataudi has taken no chances and has got Imran Khan also to say his bit about Shastri's fitness though what Imran has to do with Shastri's fitness is beyond the intelligent as well as the simpleton.

If the idea is to show that Shastri went in spite of not being fit and thus did not have the team's interests at heart, then Shastri could also turn around and ask how our bowlers who had done such a fine job earlier bowled so many loose deliveries in the matches against West Indies, New Zealand and South Africa? While batsmen get accused of playing for themselves and not for the team, how come bowlers who suddenly become generous never get questioned. In all this plotting and manoeuvring, the captain Azharuddin has kept a dignified silence and all those who have had a go at him should be thankful for that, for believe me if he opens his mouth, some players may not even be players, leave alone be captains!

Sachin and his masterful stroke.

07.05.1992

LONG CAMPS DON'T
Come with Success Guarantees

When I was just picked to play for India in 1971, the letter from the Hon. Secretary of the Cricket Board said that I should report to the manager of the Indian team at 3 pm at the Cricket Club of India for net practice. This was barely three or four days before the team flew to the West Indies. The entire team practised either in the morning or in the afternoon, mostly afternoons as those who were employed in Bombay preferred to go to their offices in the mornings and then practice in the afternoon. The practise used to be intensive but also with a bit of light-heartedness, what with fun-loving people like Dilip Sardesai, Salim Durrani and Prasanna around. It was a good mix, the players loved to pull each other's legs and as a newcomer what struck me was the informality between the established players and how they enjoyed each other's company. For practice, we also had Bombay's top bowlers, Abdul Ismail, Padmakar Shivalkar, Ajit Naik and Milind Rege to bowl to us and take the load off the Indian bowlers. The batsmen got the regular ten to twelve minutes in the nets, the bowlers bowled to four batsmen before taking a break, though bowlers like Bishen Singh Bedi and Venkatraghavan bowled to more batsmen to get their pinpoint accuracy and length. There was no physical exercise excepting a lap of the ground at the end of the practice session. Compared to today's physical workouts, the whole session was a bit of a joke but in six months, the same team had beaten West Indies and England both and that too, in their countries. These practice sessions were not compulsory and on the eve of the tour to England, there were one or two players who landed in Bombay just a day before departure and practised only for a day.

Now we have compulsory physical conditioning camps for it is a government condition that every Indian team going abroad for an international event has to have a physical conditioning camp. This was perhaps due to the fact that in mid-1970s, some Indian team (not cricket) that went out for international meets carried with them participants whose fitness was suspect even before they left India and whose subsequent performances caused embarrassment to Indian sport. The government, in order to ensure that no sports persons went on a free junket, decided that a conditioning camp for sportspersons was a must, so that not only would the players be mentally and physically prepared for the event but those who were hiding injuries would be found out and exposed and left behind and fitter persons would take their place. This was all done with the best of intentions though, of course, it would be great fun if the same kind of camps were to be held for the officials who accompany the team to see how fit administratively or otherwise they are for the job!

The result of this government directive has been that in most other sports there is an endless round of camps which leave the players in those disciplines mentally and physically fatigued while in cricket the camps in recent times have been more get-together camps like we had in 1971 than what the government actually intended. Cricket invariably gets compared to other sports and so the comments start that cricketers have it too easy and how the camps are a farce because other sports have longer and intensive camps. What people forget is that in spite of longer camps, other sports have not always delivered the results and the time has now come to have a look at the efficacy of such long camps and more importantly, at the methods that are used at these camps. There is simply no point in having these camps if the players are going to embark on the plane totally tired and listless instead of being fresh and raring to go at the competition.

Madhavrao Scindia

As far as cricket is concerned, the media takes these camps more seriously than the cricketers themselves, so everyday there is a mention of what happened at the camp, who was present, who wasn't, and who batted well and who bowled well. So when the team broke up to go play a benefit game (of cricket mind you, not chess or billiards) there was an outburst of criticism. Admittedly the entire team did not go to play the benefit game for a Dronacharya award winner but by now we know what the word commitment means to some players. It was not as if the players that went were to laze about. In fact, match practice is certainly a darn sight better than net practice, for in the nets a batsman knows that even if he gets out he will get another go and the bowler also is aware that if he bowls loosely or oversteps he will still continue to bowl. In a match, even if it is a benefit game, the players will have to keep errors to the minimum in order to carry on batting or bowling. A match, therefore, is anytime better than a net and in future it might be a good idea to have a match or two during the camp between the local state team and the Indian team, for it will also break the monotony of the camp.

After the match, some of the senior players flew off to Delhi to be briefed by the officials of the External Affairs Ministry about the conditions in South Africa and how the players should react to the situation prevalent there. Considering that India does not have a High Commission or Consulate there, this was a most vital briefing and credit should be given to the manager Amrit Mathur for foreseeing the possible problem and enlisting the help of the experts at the External Affairs Department. Because the Cricket Control Board President Madhavrao Scindia was also present at the briefing, the meeting was twisted to make it look as if he had summoned the players and he was thus blamed for disrupting the camp. This is childish, for even if the senior players are not there, it does not mean the camp cannot take place. After all, even when the senior players were around there were absentees through illness, so there was never the full contingent at practice everyday of the camp. But then Madhavrao Scindia makes a good target for those with vested interests and it is easier to point a finger at him than at nonentities, though in this particular case, the finger is absolutely wrongly pointed. Madhavrao Scindia is a politician and is used to the allegations that surface in his chosen profession. As I write this, the Indian team is struggling to avoid the follow-on against the Test debutants Zimbabwe and unless the team starts to perform better in the days ahead, Madhavrao Scindia can expect more fingers to be pointed at him than are at present.

21.10.1992

HANG ON,
Kapil Knows Best!

The recent spate of articles in some papers in the West Zone, querying Kapil Dev's position in the Indian team, are nothing but wishful thinking on the part of the writers. For, make no mistake, Kapil Dev has still a lot to contribute to Indian cricket. The articles seemed to be prompted by the fact that Kapil did not bowl at all in the first innings of the Duleep Trophy game against Central Zone. North Zone has always had a surfeit of good new-ball bowlers and more so in the last couple of years, so for Kapil to give more opportunities to his other colleagues is an action that needs to be lauded and not criticised. After all, he has nothing to prove to anyone and by allowing others to use the new ball, he is, in fact, creating more options for Indian cricket.

His wanting to conserve his energies, physical as well as mental, reminds me of the Indian tour to England in 1979. Having had a surfeit of cricket in the 1978-79 season, it became very difficult to concentrate in the tour first class matches against the counties in England. There was no trophy, no points, nothing at stake, when one played those matches, excepting getting some practice. Most counties also preferred to rest their top bowlers and keep them fresh, for their County Championships. In such a scenario, when I went out to bat, all that I was interested in was to get off the mark and then, simply throw my bat around. I had of course, mentioned my difficulty in concentrating to the skipper, Venkat, and he understood, but the problem in Indian cricket has always been, that even if players understand each other, there are enough people around, who for their own reasons, try and cause a misunderstanding.

After a few matches, where there were not many runs on the board against my name, one of the journalists went up to Venkat and put forth the idea that I was deliberately trying to sabotage the team's progress. Venkat tried to explain to him, that I had spoken about my problems in concentrating in these lesser games, but the journalist would not listen to Venkat. He then said to Venkat that if I can switch concentration off and on, why don't I prove it by playing the next day's game against Malcolm Marshall's Hampshire team and scoring runs. So even though I was originally not to play in the game, Venkat came upto me and said that he was including me in the final eleven and that, I should get a big score so that 'I could

Sunil Gavaskar playing an artful stroke.

prove the fat slob wrong and keep him quiet' (his words not mine). I did not quite see the reason why one should worry overmuch about a journalist's doubts but because Venkat has always been a good friend and seldom if ever, asked for anything, I said I'd try my best the next day. I mean, one can never make a promise about scoring and that too, when Malcom Marshall is in the opposition. The next day, after Marshall had sent Chauhan to the hospital for a suspected broken arm, I did manage to concentrate and grafted my way to a century in a little over three hours. Having thus proved my skipper right, I indulged myself a bit and went on the slog to score the next 66 runs in a little over four overs. As I returned to the pavilion, there was Venks, standing at the entrance, with his hand outstretched. Now, those who have shaken hands with him, know that he has a bone crushing grip, so I put back my gloves on and survived the handshake, as the skipper gleefully said, 'Now I'll sort the bugger out'. Needless to add, I got the okay to slog in the remaining first class matches, so long as I played my normal game in the Tests. Thereafter, on every tour, in all the first class matches the team played, I threw my bat around and thus, knowing my inability to concentrate in these practice games, the tour selection committees were good enough to pick me for only the odd practice match and leave me out for most others.

The point I am trying to make is that, there comes a time is every cricketer's life, when his physical and mental faculties get switched on only by a challenge and that too, at the highest level. It is only when it is a contest between countries or between sides that require you to play at your best, that a player gives his utmost. Today perhaps, Kapil is at that stage, where he finds only the Tests stimulating. As

I said earlier, he has nothing to prove by getting a bagful of wickets in the Duleep Trophy, so what's wrong if he is taking a break and giving others the opportunity to show their skills. North is winning and doing so easily, even without a contribution from Kapil, so there will be no complaints from North Zone either. Kapil is aware, that bowlers need to get their rhythm right and he will no doubt start to get his rhythm, when he feels he is ready for it. Having been in international cricket for fifteen years, he is the best judge of when to start trying to reach the peak. So why don't we just leave him alone and allow him to get himself right, for the big tournaments. Gratitude has always been in short supply in our country and rather than be grateful to him for his enormous contribution to Indian cricket, some are trying to pack him off. Well, knowing Kapil as I do, I can assure you he will have some news for you guys, so don't dip your pens in the ink yet.

The news, that those selected to play for India in the C.A.B. Diamond Jubilee Tournament, will miss the Duleep Trophy matches and instead, have a camp is strange, to say the least. It is hard to understand, how running or stretching and that too, in the middle of a season, is better than actual match play, in the middle. While one can understand the Indian players not being available to play for their state or Zone when they are playing for their country, it is hard to fathom why they should not be available when they are not playing for India. By not playing, they are diluting the Duleep Trophy. This kind of a break, to have a camp, does not happen anywhere else in the cricketing world and having one, only gives the impression that on their own the players do little training. I am sure that is not true, for most Indian players really work hard and particularly now that they are aware of the competition for places in the Indian team. Already there are rumours that the camp instead of starting on October 26th will start only on November 1st so as to allow the players to play a match for the earthquake relief fund on 31st so if the camp is going to be of three days' duration, is it not better instead to play the Duleep Trophy? Whatever those who decide do, let us hope that it will all come together for India on 27 November at the Eden Gardens, Calcutta!

21.10.1993

... wire; ... re Steve Bucknor ... a third umpire ... : West Indian ... d Holder was ... st batsman given ... d out by third ... e; Sachin and ... d awaiting a third ... re decision.

THIRD EYE is a Boon

When Sachin Tendulkar was a little slow in getting back to the crease in Durban, he became the first batsman in the history of Test cricket to be adjudged run-out, through the third umpire. History was created again, when the West Indian Roland Holder was declared bowled by the third umpire, after watching the slow motion action replays. The third umpire was brought into the picture, when the umpires in the middle, were unsure of what had happened and sought the help of their colleague in the TV box.

So far, the third umpire has been brought to help those in the middle with close run-out and stumping decisions and that is the reason why the West Indians were upset that the third umpire was brought in to decide on a bowled or not decision. However, their accusation of bias has no basis whatsoever, for the umpires who asked for the decision were not Indian and the slow motion replays were clear enough, so that the third umpire who was an Indian, did not have to take a marginal decision. There are those who will insist that the benefit of the doubt should go to the batsman. That thinking was valid till last year and will be valid where good TV production is not available, but if the thinking behind bringing the third umpire is to minimize errors, then it is right that it should be used wherever possible.

The only exception is the leg-before wicket decision, where because of the camera height and angle it will not be possible to correctly judge and the umpire in the middle will be the only one in a position to give the decision as he sees it. Cricket has become far more competitive and with careers on the line, it is better to use the electronic help, than make errors which could turn the game. Remember how Steve Bucknor, a much respected umpire, did not ask for the third umpire's help in spite of not being in the proper position to judge the run-out appeal against Jonty Rhodes. The batsman got the benefit of the doubt and he went on to save South Africa from total collapse in that innings. The TV replays had clearly shown that Rhodes was short of the crease and by being allowed to continue, he changed the course of the series.

India, which could have won that Test, ended up losing the series by a solitary Test and thus strengthening the case for third umpires to be used as frequently as possible. Yes, there is a chance that the TV might not be in a position to capture every bit of the action and in such cases, where the third umpire also is unsure of what has happened, then the benefit of the doubt should go to the batsman. Apart from decisions involving dismissals, the third umpire should also come in for those saves made on the boundary line, where sometimes even the fielder is not aware that he has touched or crossed the boundary line. After all, even a run can make the difference between a victory and a defeat, or a batsman scoring 99 and a century. There is plenty at stake in international cricket today, as can be seen in the difference between the winners' and the losers' cheques and thus, all the more reason

to ensure that errors are minimized and the players have only themselves to blame and not the umpires. For, far too long, teams have got away with their own inadequacies, by pointing to the umpires and not being honest enough to look at their own performances, but the third umpire's introduction to all the decisions referred to, by those umpires in the middle, will go a long way in ridding cricket of the perennial cry babies.

Interestingly, Richie Richardson, the West Indian captain, on arrival in Sri Lanka, has said that he regards countries preparing wickets to suit the home team's strengths as a form of cheating. Perhaps, he was a little too hard with the word, but there is some merit in what he is saying. Obviously, what the West Indian skipper is objecting to, are wickets that start turning from day one of the Test match. The essence of international competition is to be able to master different conditions, in different countries. That is what separates the

Another West Indian master batsman, Richie Richardson.

great players from the good players. Having said that, one must also take into account, that the spectators come to see good cricket and if they, in watching good cricket, are also able to see a victory for their team, then, it is a bonus.

Good cricket can be seen on wickets where there is a proper balance between bat and ball. When countries prepare wickets to suit their strengths and invariably, it is bowling strength that one talks about, then the balance gets tilted in favour of the ball and this is what Richardson is objecting to. To ensure that wickets are not doctored to suit the home team's strengths, will mean that the match referee that the ICC has, will have additional work to do, unless of course, the ICC sends a specialist in pitches, all round the world. In any case, what can he or even the match referee do, if the wicket is in fact doctored by the home team. He cannot possibly declare the result null and void, and making a report to the ICC, after the match is over, is hardly going to make a difference, to the result already obtained.

The West Indies skipper has certainly given food for a lot of thought to those that run cricket and coming from the captain of a team, which wins even in alien conditions, it is certainly worth chewing over. Remember, he is not complaining about the natural conditions, like the unpredictable weather in England or the heat and dust of the subcontinent, or the searing heat of Brisbane, followed by rain the next session. These are conditions beyond the control of the home authorities. What Richardson is asking, is for some sort of uniformity in wickets, with the gradual wear and tear over the days of Test match, instead of the ball whizzing past the batsman's nose or turning from leg to first slip on the first day. It is an interesting point that he has made, though he may not have chosen the correct way to express it and considering that he is a thoughtful person not given to making statements, it is something to ponder over. A lot of the amendments or changes in the Laws of Cricket, in recent time, have been made to stifle the strength of the West Indies, so now that the West Indies skipper has a point to improve the game, then it is for the authorities to not only listen to him, but to think hard if it can be implemented, in a way so that the world of cricket can benefit.

02.12.1993

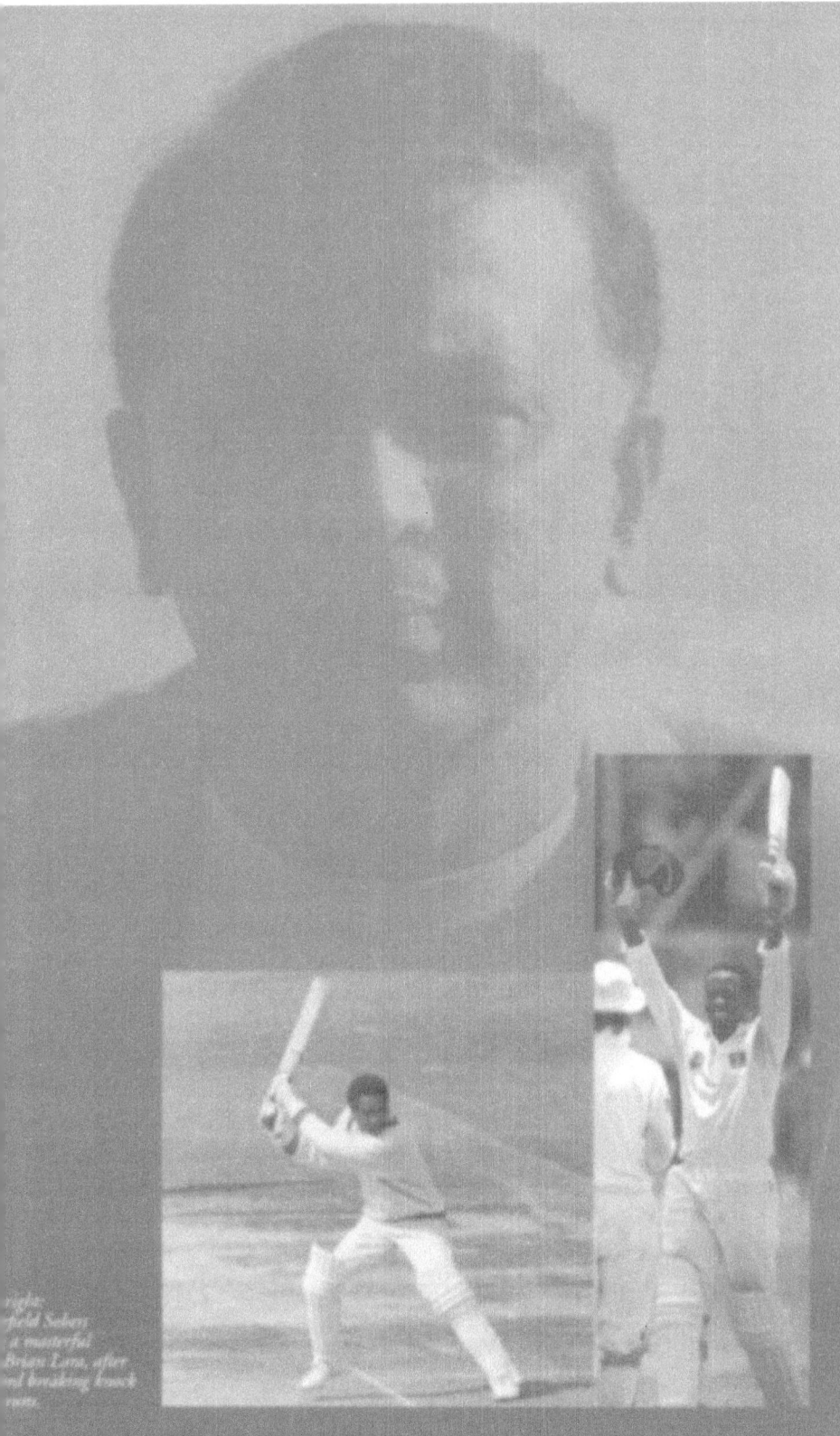

right:
field Sobers
a masterful
Brian Lara, after
d breaking knock
runs.

LARA Has Only Just Begun

Brian Lara's stupendous batting which saw him eclipse Sir Garfield Sobers' mark of 365 runs was not just the cricketing achievement of the week but perhaps will be the achievement of the decade unless, of course, someone else does better than him. We are still in the first half of the decade so who knows what kind of talent is, round the corner, so to speak, just waiting for the opportunity to show his skills. But till then it is this cricketing deed which will be the greatest deed of the decade.

Last year, when he was run out for 277 against Australia, he was inconsolable for he had set his sights on scoring 366 runs. A cricketer knows that such big scoring chances do not come often but in Lara's case, it came after barely a year and this time, he did not miss. A chanceless one it was too, and that is even more remarkable for over a long time like that a chance or two is pretty normal. That he did not offer one, shows how complete his mastery over the attack must have been. Of all the records in the cricketing world, this was the one that looked infallible, for today's cricket is such that big hundreds are not scored as often as in the past. Yes, you do have centuries but double centuries are not as frequently scored as in the old days nor of course, the triple century which is even rarer.

Lara's batting is such that of all the young batsmen in the world, he looked likely to be the one to do so, as also one likely to come agonisingly close to it for he plays shots with a rare abandon and this was likely to get him out, for a batsman who plays shots like he does, is always giving the bowler a chance. He is perhaps not as technically organised as Tendulkar and earlier in the series, the West Indian manager Rohan Kanhai was very worried because Lara was moving too far across his stumps and trying to whip every ball to the onside. It had led to his dismissal in the first Test as well as in the One-dayers and Kanhai was agonising whether to have a word with him or not. That the two of them get along very well is known in cricketing circles and Lara has tremendous respect for one of the finest West Indian batsmen of all time. One is pretty certain that Rohan Kanhai must have been telling him to keep going and keep concentrating every time he came into the dressing room for the lunch or tea break. If it was an Englishman who had achieved the feat, then you can be sure there would have been a few articles as to how the

West Indian great Rohan Kanhai executing an impossible hook shot.

England manager helped the batsman to achieve the feat but of course another manager will hardly get the same kind of credit.

Lara, Tendulkar, Kambli, Inzamam-ul-Haq, Basit Ali are some of the exciting young batsmen in the world today. Michael Slater and Justin Langer are two Aussies who will also get plenty of runs in international cricket. The one distinguishing feature of all these batsmen is their refusal to be cowed down by bowling. There are plenty of critics of the One-day game; but what the game has done is to give the batsmen confidence in their ability to play shots off any bowler. This they can translate even in the longer version of the game and that is the reason why we see more sixes and boundaries today. That is also the reason not many double hundreds are scored because batsmen who play shots are always going to give the bowler a chance by taking a risk too many. Yet, there is no denying that cricket is far more exciting today than, say, ten years back. There certainly are more results in Tests today because of the One-day game, since batsmen get out trying to play shots which they have learnt in the limited overs game.

Sir Garfield Sobers was present when Lara went past his mark and was the first to congratulate him. Those who have seen Sobers bat will always say that Lara has a long way to go to achieve the greatness of Sir Gary. But comparison in sport is odious and definitely so, when it comes to comparing players of different generations. In any case, statistics will eventually show who has achieved what and I firmly believe that statistics over a period of time are the best indicators of class, though they can sometimes be misleading in the case of a short career. Lara's has just begun though he has been in the West Indian team since 1989 when India toured the Caribbean Islands. It is only since Richards' retirement that Lara has got a regular place in the West Indian team. The one person sad at Lara's dismissal must have been Shivnarine Chanderpaul, for if Lara had continued then Chanderpaul also would have had the opportunity to go on to get his first Test century. Lara's dismissal meant that Walsh promptly closed the innings to have a go at the English batsmen, since it was already well into the third day, when Lara got past the record, though the English batsmen must be given credit for not wilting under the pressure that day itself.

Hopefully, Lara's record will egg on the other contenders to the throne of being the best batsmen in the world; to go on to post by scores for their countries and if this rivalry continues, then the world's bowlers will have to look for another way to spend the time of the day, for bowling to broad bats and chasing leather is not the best way of spending the day. There is no doubt that while there are plenty of young batsmen in the world, the same cannot be said of bowlers. There is, of course, Shane Warne and Anil Kumble and Waqar Younis who are all in their early twenties but they are all invariably playing lone hands for their teams while the young batsmen have one or two good batsmen in their teams, as well as some experienced senior batsmen too. The pressure on them is, thus, that much less than on the younger bowlers, who not only have no bowlers to share their burden of taking wickets but also not many to keep pressure on from the other end.

So, shall we see more and more batting records set in the next few years? The answer has to be yes though it is difficult to say whether the mark of 375 will be the one that will be broken. Or shall we say that this record will survive this century? And the next?

21.04.1994

WHY DOES ANYONE
Have to be a Bradman

B rian Lara's stupendous run with the bat has now taken him to the peak of the first class record for batting. With the Test batting record already under his belt, Brian now is without doubt the best batsman in the world. After all, just as the proof of the pudding is in the eating, the proof of ability in sports is on the scoreboard and Lara certainly has kept the scorers and scoreboard operators busy. Seven centuries in eight innings is what even Sir Don Bradman never scored, yet there are some who ask 'Is Lara another Bradman?' Why? Why does anybody have to be a Bradman? Why can't Lara simply be Lara? Sir Don with his fantastic average is always going to be the yardstick by which batsmen will be compared but I think it is about time people realised that there is a world of difference between the cricket played in the 1920s and 1930s and the cricket being played in the 1990s. Old timers love to go into a time warp and relive the days when they were young and the world belonged to them, but there are also old timers who move on with the times and are practical about present-day sport and achievements. Sir Len Hutton was one such and I remember watching a Test with him at Lord's, when David Gower at cover, dived to his right and cut off what would have been a certain boundary. Sir Len turned to me and said, 'This is the difference between our days and present-day cricket. It is much harder to find the gaps now, what with such athletic fielding. I don't think we would have been able to score the same amount of runs as we did!' Now whether Sir Len was being modest about his own achievements or whether he was just playing along with a current cricketer (I was still playing then) is not very sure, for Sir Len did have a very dry sense of humour and often it went over one's head. Sir Don has said that a champion in one era would have been a champion in any era and there is no disputing that, for there is no question that the thing that separates the champions from the other participants is the ability to adapt to different conditions, and still come out on top. Sir Don will remain the greatest batsman ever in the world, until someone comes along who will score runs with the same appetite, and make bowlers wish they were somewhere else, and do it consistently over his career. Lara's career has just begun and he is getting into that consistency level now, but whether he will be able to maintain it, we will have to wait and see. Till then, let Lara be Lara. Let us not provoke the West Indians like they were provoked in the 1930s, when George Headley was reeling off hundred after hundred. When reports began appearing in the papers that Headley was the 'Black Bradman', proud Jamaicans began to call Bradman 'The White Headley'.

That is the difference between West Indians and Indians. You can be sure that if it was an Indian who had scored 501 not out, there would be quite a few Indians who would have said that the attack was a lollipop attack, so what's the big deal? Some would have said that the Indian was playing for records when the match could have been made interesting by an earlier declaration. Some would have criticized just for the heck of it and in order to be different. If we are good at one thing, it is running down our achievers. Have you ever found unanimity in the appreciation of achievements? There will always, always be someone who casts doubts, casts aspersions on the achievement and especially if the achievement means a foreigner has been surpassed or overtaken. And it does not even have to be a world record achievement. Any achievement will find its detractors. That is the Indian speciality! That is an aspect at which we are champions. Absolutely unbeatable there.

The entire Caribbean community which comprises different nations have taken Brian Lara to their heart and believe that his record is their own record. They are fiercely proud of him and there is not a voice of dissent about his achievements. Even before he got to these records, people in the Caribbean believed he was the best batsman in the world, though he did not have the consistency to be considered thus. The one question that ordinary people in West Indies asked me regularly was whether Tendulkar was better than Lara. At that time, there was no question in my mind that the young Indian champion with his technique and temperament was the better player, but the West Indians would hoot the suggestion out, with the typical rocking laughter that they have. I also pointed out to them that I had never seen Tendulkar being discomfited by the short ball like Lara had been by Malcolm in the first Test. Lara was fending the ball off his face in an ugly manner and then asked for some eye ointment to be brought out.

The point is, he was batting at the other end quite comfortably and did not seem to need the ointment then. With the kind of consistency Lara has shown there is no question that he is the best in the world today and Tendulkar will have to get really big scores to wrest that title from him. The reason, I suspect, Tendulkar does not get big hundreds is because if he finds that there is no challenge in the bowling, he gets bored and tries something different and it is in this effort that he gets out.

Remember his dismissal after that electrifying innings in New Zealand, when he was promoted to open the batting for the first time. Tendulkar has to make the best of his youth when everything is going for him, ambition, energy, stamina. After a certain time, all these start to diminish and record-setting becomes difficult. Most batsmen or bowlers have recorded their best figures before they are twenty-five, after which it becomes difficult, not impossible, just difficult. Tendulkar must get ruthless when has the bowlers at his mercy and score as many as he can, for there has been many a cricketer who at the end of his career has lamented the fact that he did not score more when he was younger, or go on to take more wickets only because he found no batsman worth bowling to.

Lara's scores should be the motivating factor for both Tendulkar and Kambli. Kambli, after his brilliant start, let himself down by getting out when well set against Sri Lankans in India and if it was the question of over-confidence, hopefully he will realise that a batsman has to commit just one mistake to be back in the pavilion. He missed out on what were almost certain centuries or more and I am sure he must have been kicking himself after those outs.

Uday Pawar's open letter to me just proves the point I made in my earlier column, that sportspersons from other disciplines have not always supported each other, while making their demands. His examples of players making out of court settlements, etc., show that unlike the cricketers who stick together, in spite of their differences, badminton players have not been able to do so. The reason I mentioned Pargat Singh and Sanjay Sharma is because these two have spoken out more than once, but have had little or no support from others in their sport. This is not to suggest that other sportspersons do not care about their sport only because they are silent but their support would have made a difference. Uday himself had taken the Badminton Federation to court, but it is obvious that his main objection seems to be that I mentioned only Sanjay Sharma who Uday feels has played up to the officials, when he was an active player. Ours is a free country and Uday is perfectly entitled to have a go at Sanjay Sharma, if he believes Sanjay has not been consistent in his support for players' causes. But not over my shoulder please!

16.06.1994

India captain
Sardar Singh
and Dilip
Vengsarkar
at the Wankhede

C'MON BCCI, Give Them a 100

This is being written a couple of days before the first Test at Bombay. The phone continues to ring with people calling up and asking for tickets for the match. Of course, the tickets they want are complimentary tickets, though some who call are capable of buying the entire stand up, at the snap of their fingers. But getting complimentary tickets is somehow a status symbol. What they do not know is that complimentary tickets are not necessarily the best seats. The best seats to watch a game at the Wankhede Stadium are in the 'G' Block of Garware Pavilion or the Tata stand or North stand as it is popularly called.

Now that I am no longer a player I do not get any complimentary tickets, apart from the two seats for my wife and I, which the Bombay Cricket Association very graciously reserved for us in the 'G' Block of Garware Pavilion, after my retirement. I understand that this year the BCA Managing Committee has decided to give some more tickets to Dilip Vengsarkar, Ajit Wadekar, Sandeep Patil and myself, which is indeed very nice of them though, irrespective of the number of tickets they give you, it simply isn't enough in your home town, as any current player would agree.

A current player gets complimentary tickets, plus he can buy tickets on a priority basis. The number of complimentary tickets at each centre varies per player, depending on whether it is his state or zone, in which the game is being played. The normal practice is to split the tickets equally between the players. The Board's rules state that each centre will supply seventy-five complimentary tickets to the team. These tickets are then split between the members of the team. With the Indian team comprising fourteen players, plus manager and physio, it would work out to four tickets per player, with the manager deciding what to do with the extra eleven tickets he will have left with him. Normally he will give it to some important people, as also to players from the state or the zone where the game is held. Players too will have an understanding among themselves, so that they give their tickets to the players from the venue state, in turn for getting tickets from the player when the match is in their home town.

Why the complimentary tickets to the team have been reduced from 100 to 75 is not known, for in 1979 the team used to get 100 'complis'. That season the Indian

The historical Wankhede Stadium.

team used to comprise twelve players plus manager, so it would work out seven complimentary tickets per player and manager. The balance nine tickets would be given to the players from the venue state/zone. Dilip Doshi, who was the only player from the East Zone, would thus get the extra nine tickets for the Calcutta Test, but he was good enough to split them with some who needed them.

The Board should consider going back to giving 100 complimentary tickets to the Indian team, for that will mean that each player will get atleast six tickets. If a player is married and has to bring his parents as well as in-laws to the game, then six tickets is the minimum that he will need. The reason why giving more complimentary tickets is being advocated is very simple: the pressure on a current player for tickets is enormous, and if he is going to get worried about how he will get them, then his practice before the game is affected, because his mind is on how to satisfy all those who need tickets. It is not only the family that he has to look after, but also those who have helped him in his career, like his coach, teachers, friends, etc. The present set of four complimentary tickets each, is simply not enough. Far better to give a player more tickets, and have him relaxed before a big game, rather than him rushing about to get tickets to satisfy everybody who makes a call on him.

Most Test centres give their Ranji players as well as former players one complimentary ticket each, but not all centres give visiting former Indian players a ticket. If one has played for the country, then one should be entitled to a complimentary ticket anywhere one goes to watch a game, and if one needs a few more, one should be given that as well.

The current Board president gets fifty complimentary tickets at each venue, and the other office-bearers get slightly less number according to their place in the hierarchy. Besides the president's Box, there is also the Cricket Control Box, which again has plenty of invitees. The players' wives sometimes are lucky to be guests of these Boxes. But while these tickets to current office bearers is understandable, because of the demands made on them due to the popularity of the game, what is hard to understand is why former presidents of the Board should be given ten complimentary tickets, former secretaries and treasurers eight complis and so on, while former Indian cricketers get only one for themselves. And this they get at every centre and not just at their home centre. If former Board presidents, who have been in office for three years, can get ten complimentary tickets, surely a former player who has sweated and toiled for the country should get more than one. And remember, the current player whom the crowds come to see is lucky to get only four when he is actually participating in the match. Can you think of anything more absurd than this state of affairs? One is not begrudging the former officials what they get, but if they are deemed to have made a contribution and thus get rewarded, so also a player who has played for the country should be rewarded. After all, even he would have people expecting him to get tickets for them. The Board can draw up a scheme, where players who have played for the country for a number of Tests, would get tickets according to a slab system. This will save the former player the embarrassment of queuing up for tickets outside officials' offices or home.

Mr. Bindra and Mr. Dalmiya's aim, since they took office, is to give dignity to even the unknown first class player, for he too is a contributor to Indian cricket. They have brought in money to supplement and strengthen the first class game in the country. Yet, the pervading feeling in Indian cricket is that the official behind the scenes is superior to the man on the field. If in the remainder of their term, they can get rid of this feeling then that will be their greatest contribution to Indian cricket.

16.11.1994

and Gavaskar
during their
... The champ
Gavaskar

In memory of **PUMKAKA**

The Wills World Cup is over. After more than a month of frenetic activity and travelling, there is a feeling of emptiness now. India's first failure to win the cup was bad enough, but to lose a very dear relative is worse. Two days after the last ball had been bowled in the Wills World Cup, the umpire above, signaled Pramod Pandit out. 'Pumkaka' as I and everyone else called him, lived and breathed for cricket. My father was brought up by 'Pumkaka's' parents and I spent the first eighteen years of my life in the Pandit house before we moved out. 'Pumkaka' was probably the greatest Australian supporter ever and I wouldn't be surprised to know that it was the trauma of 'his team's' loss in the finals that brought about the massive heart attack that claimed his life.

He was the one who introduced Milind Rege (who lived in the same complex then) and me to the international names in cricket. As schoolboys, we had little idea about who was who in international cricket, but 'Pumkaka' not only knew that but also every statistic about cricketers. We used to play tennis ball cricket in the cramped space between the staircases, and the Sunday afternoon tennis ball matches between two teams formed from the residents of the complex used to be looked forward to events and even attract passersby who used to be fascinated by the intensity with which these matches were played. It is amazing how many Indians are great Australian supporters but I have yet to come across anybody who was as fanatical an Australian supporter as 'Pumkaka' so much so that even when India played Australia during the time I played, he would want me to get a century but would not want the Indian team to win. If I wrote anything critical of Australia, he would complain good-naturedly to his friends saying 'see what my nephew is writing'. His passing away is not only an irreparable personal loss to me but to the game of cricket, especially Australian cricket has lost one of its greatest supporters.

Talking of supporters, the Sri Lankan victory has brought forward many supporters in that country to offer rewards to the members of the team that brought glory to the country. There have been cars, holidays offered apart from the financial rewards as well, all thoroughly deserved, of course, for the Sri Lankans played some brilliant aggressive cricket and their tactics of going for max not only in the last fifteen but also the first fifteen overs signals a new tactic in limited overs

Gavaskar – the famous stance.

cricket. Hopefully, the Sri Lankan players will get all that is being offered to them unlike what happened to the World Cup winning Indian team of 1983.

Immediately after that unbelievable victory, there were many who climbed onto the bandwagon of those announcing prizes and rewards to the Indian team. Unfortunately, all that these people wanted was someone who announced that his company would give rice to the members of the Indian team for the rest of their lives. Someone else announced that his company's beer would be given every week or so, someone else announced free medicines. The list of all those wanting to make announcements was so long, that nobody had the time to even stop and think whether these were genuine offers or just people trying to link their company's name and thus get free publicity. Predictably, apart from the Cricket Control Board's announcements and some State government announcements, none of the other announcements was fulfilled. News of all these announcements had spread over the world and the West Indians, who lost that final, were grumbling that even when they won the first two World Cups they had received not a penny more than the actual prize money. It was only after they were told in 1987 when they came for the Reliance World Cup that all those announcements were fake that they felt they had not been hard done by their Board and the West Indian public.

This Wills World Cup was no different and the number of people and companies who tried to associate themselves indirectly was amazing, to say the least. They all knew that the attention of the subcontinent was going to be focused on the game and so they found some way or the other to get involved. If they could not get official status because the fees asked for that were way out of their budget, then they got into it by some way or the other. So you saw a photograph of Kapil holding that Prudential Cup or photos of the players during the prize distribution ceremony with some catching caption that caught the attention. There were some products like TVs that linked themselves to the World Cup action and thus got mileage for themselves. So long as these were advertisements that were paid for, it was fine but when speculation started about the kind of money the players were getting or about the Cola wars, the figures quoted became fanciful each day.

Today, of course, it is more glamorous to attach figures in terms of crores and not in lakhs and if one paper said one figure, another had to either double or triple it without even verifying whether any of the figures were true. Not just the players but even some companies who were on the periphery of the marketing of the event were reported to be making crores when it is not even a fraction of that figure. As I said, the bigger the figure the more glamorous it looks and the more eye-catching the article becomes and the hell with the truth. Adding a few zeroes to the figure is so easy that one wishes a zero could have been added to the double digit scores of two of our batsmen in the semifinals, for then it would have been the Indian team receiving all the awards that the Sri Lankan team is supposedly receiving.

So let a few months pass, let the euphoria die down and then we will know from the Sri Lankan cricketers if their countrymen were genuine in putting their money where their mouths were or were they too like the Indians in 1983 when it came to putting their hands in their pockets.

21.03.1996

legend Indian
Former Indian
jit Wadekar,
th African and
n coach Bob
r, English legend
llingworth.

ULTIMATELY,
Man-Management Matters

B ob Woolmer, the South African coach, is an interesting person to talk to. Like all cricket coaches, he is an animated talker and can go on endlessly about the techniques and temperament required to be a top class cricketer. Coaches have to be in love with the game without which it is virtually impossible to pass on the knowledge and experience one has, to those wanting to learn. Bob played for England for a few years and he was a pretty useful player though he will be the first to admit that he was not a great player. Having come up through the English system, he believes that technique is important but that temperament has an equal place too. He carries with him a laptop computer into which he feeds the data of the matches that the South Africans play, and of how not only the South African players have performed but also the opposition. This enables him to go back to any game and find out who did what and in which manner. He also has gathered video cassettes of the top batsmen and bowlers of his generation and the previous ones, so that he can tell the youngsters how they played and show them on the video what made those players top players then.

Today, of course, coaches or cricket managers of national teams have to do much more than just tell players about their technical shortcomings. They also have to be motivators and try and get every player to perform to the best of his ability. So, before the Sharjah tournament began, Woolmer had each player come up to his room individually and he brought out with the help of his laptop the performances of the player during the season and especially in the Wills World Cup. He then talked to the player about his performance and told him where he could improve. More importantly, he told him that if he did not improve there was every possibility of him being dropped when the new season began. This way he not only got the player to know what he had done but what he had to do to stay in the team. Now one does not know whether Woolmer is part of the selection committee in South Africa but even if he is not, his word must carry enough weight for him to be able to tell each player what is expected of him and the consequences if the efforts to attain that were not enough. South Africa has dropped many players who have performed well but have lost form and that is one way of ensuring nobody, absolutely nobody, becomes complacent and takes his place in the team for granted. In India and

Pakistan, one good performance virtually ensures that player a place in the team for a season, if not more, and when a player feels complacent then you can be sure that consistency will go out of the window.

India's most successful manager, Ajit Wadekar, may not have used the laptop to feed in information about his team and the opposition, but with his quick grasp of a situation he was able to ensure that the Indian team had the right answers to the position that they found themselves in. He was also able to get the players to respond to him for he had that low-key, self-mocking approach that won the players' loyalty. His code of conduct which he imposed on the players was much talked about and though in later years he did not insist on it, he implemented it at a time the players needed to be focused and not distracted from the game. He may not have been a technical advisor to the team but in his own unique way, he motivated the team to play well and the results under his managership tell their own story.

The current Indian cricket manager, Sandeep Patil, has naturally a hard act to follow Ajit Wadekar, but he has his own views and because he is younger than Wadekar the players are already calling him 'Sandybhai' rather then 'Sir' as Wadekar was referred to. Sandeep is also more of a motivator than a theoretician and the way he turned around Madhya Pradesh and made them into a team that believed in itself shows what a fine motivator he is.

Ray Illingworth was the best captain that I have seen. He was such an instinctive reader of the game and such a shrewd captain that to win against England then meant that a team had to be really good and also have a great good fortune. As the cricket manager too, he brought about a change in the thinking of the English team so much so that England managed to hold West Indies to a drawn series last season. Somehow he seemed to have lost that touch during the England's tour of South Africa and then of course in the Wills World Cup and England were back to performing below par again. Perhaps the British media was far too intrusive and did not allow Atherton and Illingworth to settle down and that is crucial, for, if a captain and the manager do not hit off, then the team is in trouble as we have seen in India itself.

Bobby Simpson is the longest serving cricket manager and though he said that he would quit when he knew that the Australian team no longer needs a cricket manager, he is still around. Perhaps Simpson feels that in spite of the Australians being the unofficial World Champions in Test Cricket and official runner-up in One-day cricket, his services are still required. He has had his detractors in the media—and that too former players—but he is going like Old Man River.

His strength has been his belief in fielding being the key to a team's success. He has devised ways and means to make cricket fielding practice interesting so that the players do not feel jaded or go through a regular routine that takes away enthusiasm so necessary to have a meaningful practice. Under his managership, the Australians have grown to be one of the top teams in the world. They have been very consistent in their performances and have been feared opponents not only for their determined approach but also for the way they are flexible enough to combat situation they find themselves in.

The other manager who has been around for a long time is Intikhab Alam and he too is more of a motivator than a person who lays emphasis on technique. His has had a mixed tenure but Pakistan is not a team that anybody takes lightly ever, for they have some brilliant players even though they can be temperamental at times.

In the end, though, it is the players who have to perform on the field and you could have your theoreticians and motivators as managers but if the players do not do their job then the managers can only wring their hands or tear their hair out in despair. That is a darn sight easier to do than to throw your laptop computer as Bob Woolmer may have been tempted to do after they lost in the Wills World Cup!!

19.04.1996

OUR OWN Sachin Tendulkar

'He plays in a similar manner. It is just his compactness and his stroke production that make me feel that I must have played in much the same manner!' This was how the greatest batsman of them all, Sir Don Bradman, described our own Sachin Tendulkar. The papers in England, especially the old-time writers like John Woodcock and E.W. Swanton have gone into raptures over The Don's comments and having seen The Don bat, and now Sachin play one of the finest Test century innings ever, they are in full agreement with The Greatest. Woodcock has gone even further and is confident that having seen the way our little champion carries himself on and off the field, he will be as unspoilt by success as The Don was.

Family background and upbringing has a large part to play in a successful person keeping his head on his shoulders and feet firmly on the ground and with a professor as a father, and a brother who writes fine poetry in his spare time, Sachin would in due course live up to not only Woodcock's hopes, but those of all Indians and cricket lovers around the world. We must not forget, of course his wife, Anjali, who is the big stabilising factor for him and who has inherited the dry British wit from her mother. She will have a harder time coping with the adulation that her husband attracts and being a doctor and a paediatrician at that, she can always be on hand if her baby-faced husband begins to get a little too big at the corners and give him a not so gentle tap on the head to get it back into shape. Today, the whole of India adores Sachin but make no mistake, the moment he assumes the captaincy of India he will have a few disgruntled people having their own peculiar reasons for not warming to him.

Six years ago, on the eve of his departure to England in 1990, I had been invited by the other residents of the co-operative society where he lives, to be the chief guest at the good luck farewell function they were having for him. I remember saying then, that his voice sounded (it still does) like Sir Don Bradman's and I hoped that he would be able to do a bit like Sir Don did on his first tour of England. At that time Sachin did not even have a Test century to his name and there were some who thought I was getting a bit carried away. But now with Sir Donald himself paying him the ultimate accolade, I guess I am not too far wrong.

Sachin Tendulkar with his better half, Anjali.

In our commentary box every single commentator (including Charles Colville, who is as staunch a British supporter as one could hope to see) are big admirers of him and want to see him do well.

The only person he seems to annoy is Ian Botham and that too only when Sachin calls him Mr. Botham, while Ian wants him to call him by his nickname 'Beefy'! But in this case, Sachin is doing exactly what I have told him to do for an annoyed Botham is of more value than a mellow one. Even Botham was touched, when Sachin on his way to a BBC TV interview stopped and said to me 'Sir, that first raising of the bat was for you and then to the dressing room.' How can you but not like the man who in his moment of glory has the time to remember the few moments spent in the morning, talking technique. Not that one is trying to take credit for his superb batting, but it is always a pleasure to talk to him when he approaches one for having told him of some minor adjustments needed, and one can see him making the effort to correct himself.

Two other eager to learn players are Jadeja and Rathore and though they do not have the skills of our little champion, they are both brave and gutsy players with good temperament. The others seem to be more keen on the foreign label syndrome and going to players from other countries for advice or tips. Not that they should not go to them but when former Indian players like Amarnath, Vengsarkar, Shastri are available, why not pick their brains for tips and advice. After all they have seen more of the Indian players, even before these players came into the Test team, and so would be more aware of their technique and the slight changes that occur unknown to the players themselves.

All of us are Indians and we dearly want our team to do well and are available if our experience is required in any way. If our observation in our media roles are at times critical, that is simply because we know that the players have more potential and are capable of more. Our observations are in the hope that the team will play better and not because we get any special pleasure out of writing something critical. It is disappointing to see players not playing upto the potential they have because of carelessness or lack of cricketing thinking. But it is even more disappointing to be slotted as anti a particular player or two, for at the cost of repeating oneself, we are keen to see the team do well and bring glory to the country. If ever Sandeep Patil or Azhar want to pick on our experience all that they have to do is walk up like Tendulkar did and so regularly does, and we would be only too happy to be of help.

All the help will, of course, be of no use if the umpires make the mistakes they do. In the first One-day game at the Oval, Tendulkar was chopped off just when he looked good and the Test match could have gone either way if Hussein had been given out caught off his gloves. Umpires from Australia seem to get more decisions wrong for catches behind the wicket than other umpires. In all the Test matches involving India, since third country umpiring started officially, I have yet to see a decision that has benefited India but can reel off instances of the ones that have allowed the opposition to recover and then beat India. There are of course, reports to be filled up on the umpires by captains, managers and the ICC Match referee but as yet, one has not heard about umpires being dropped from the ICC panel due to bad reports all round. It does sound like a chummy club much like the Indian team, though I guess Kambli, Prabhakar and now, Navjot Singh Sidhu will not agree!

13.06.1996

TIGER, Tiger So Bright

The green jacket! That is the ultimate in golf for that is what the winner of the U.S. Masters Tournament in Augusta gets. I am no golf addict like some of my former cricketing colleagues are. So I could be wrong about the U.S. Masters being the ultimate Golf Championship. Nevertheless it was fascinating to watch Tiger Woods win it at his first attempt after turning professional and he did it not only in style but setting up several records in the process. He was so far ahead on the final day that it was a foregone conclusion that there would be no one else coming even close to him. All that he needed to do was to ensure that he played naturally and he would win by a record margin, which he did. His concentration was phenomenal and added to that was the magnificence of his hitting while his putting was awesome to put it mildly.

Before the tournament started, all talk in the electronic media was about whether he would be able to win it. Champions like Nick Faldo, Greg Norman and even legendary Jack Nicklaus felt that though Tiger had the talent he did not have the experience that is needed to win at Augusta. Previous history had shown that only three other golfers had won it at their first attempt and it took many years of participation for some others to win it. Now Faldo, Norman and Nicklaus know their golf for they are all great champions but perhaps their observation that all Tiger needed was a little more experience may have been just a little bit of gamesmanship, since they too were competing and may not have wanted to give him any psychological advantage. But when temperament is allied to skill, there is no stopping a sportsperson especially someone as talented as Tiger Woods.

Watching him play, one could not help but compare him and Tendulkar. Both are hugely talented, both have the same unflappable temperament. They are extremely popular wherever they play and of course they are not short of wealth. They carry themselves with dignity not only on their respective playing arenas but also off it and are wonderful ambassadors for their sport and ideal role models for the youngsters. They have it in them to rewrite the record books and while Tiger has already begun with this win at Augusta, Tendulkar has so far only whetted one's appetite and kept us waiting for the main course. Not for one moment am I suggesting that Tendulkar should play for records, for, believe me, nobody can play for records for they simply happen and it is only those who have never played at the highest level who will say of others that they are playing for records. The pressure and tension of playing at the highest level is so intense that no sane person would add to it by playing for a record. What someone as gifted as Tendulkar or Woods has to do is to not let that talent down by not fully applying themselves whenever they are playing and thus eventually playing below their best. In Golf, of course, a player is playing against himself but in cricket there are other eleven players if one is a batsman like Tendulkar is!

That Sachin Tendulkar in spite of being in Test cricket since late 1989 has not yet got a double century against his name is an indication that while the talent is there perhaps the application is not always the same. Unfortunately, time does not wait for anybody and though the peak years of a batsman are normally from twenty-seven to thirty-three years, it is the early twenties when he is really, really hungry for runs and more importantly, has the energy for it. If you look at most of the records in cricket for individuals, they have all come about when the player has been in his early twenties rather than later. Tiger Woods and Sachin Tendulkar are special people and we are truly fortunate that today with satellite television we can watch them play anywhere in the world.

From the green jacket to the green T-shirt. That is the uniform of the 'Trini' posse that travels around the Caribbean islands supporting the West Indian team. The green T-shirt is actually their travelling shirt, which they use only when they are flying from one centre to another, and both Ravi Shastri and I were questioned by the leader of the Trini Posse at the Barbados airport why we were not wearing those since they had earlier presented the shirt to the commentators during the previous Test. Since they had given me a double XL shirt, there was no way I was going to wear it. I mean I wanted to fly, not float! But seeing the whole group (Posse) at the airport in their travel shirts brought a query in my mind as to why India in spite of its huge cricket following has not yet got a band of supporters who will travel to various centres, albeit in India, to cheer for their heroes. England has its 'barmy army' who travel not only within England but all over the world and in fact they are now a registered entity. They have their own uniforms, caps, bags and what started as a lark is now becoming a good business. They now get sponsorships from airlines etc. because they get covered a lot on TV.

Surely somebody in India can also form a supporters group to go around and shout for their team. Two names come to mind of people who can do it, for not only are they sportspersons themselves but also great lovers of all sports. But whether their business interest will allow them to do so is the question.

But if they do so, it will not only mean a lot of fun but also good mileage and coverage for their respective businesses and fairly inexpensive too! I refer to Vijay Mallya and Gautam Singhania. Both travel a lot to watch sports, are keen competitive sportsmen themselves and most important, they have the kind of friends who will enliven a dull day's game. They know the Indian players too, so to have an evening or two out with the players would not be a problem and be relaxing for the players as well, but they are busy people and whether their huge business commitments will give them the time is a big question. But if they do, then India can have its own army of Posse!

17.04.1997

INDIAN BADMINTON
Could See the Light

Prakash Padukone's decision to head the Indian Badminton Federation could not have come at a better time for the sport. There are many who will contend that it was long overdue but Prakash has always given the impression of a person who takes his time to decide but once he does he gives it everything. He is also known for avoiding situations that can lead to a controversy, so his decision to head a parallel body to the Badminton Association of India means quite simply that even he too lost patience with the powers that have been running the game of badminton in our country for the last several decades.

There has been plenty of criticism about the way the Badminton Association of India functioned but while it has been talked about it has led to no improvement and the officials have blithely carried on. They have carried on simply because of the way the constitution of the association has been framed which allows them to do so for years on end and this is true of other sporting federations as well, whether they are national or state level associations. No wonder they call themselves democratically elected but conveniently forget to add who are the ones who elect them.

What sort of democracy are we talking about when the voters are your own drivers, cooks, peons, clerks and personal assistants. This kind of democracy is not democracy at all for those who depend upon you for their livelihood are hardly likely to vote against you. To this claim that you are democratically elected is to throw dust in the eyes of the casual observer. If at all a public interest litigation is ever necessary, it is to examine the way the national federation and state associations take upon themselves the right to govern the sport. It is needed to find out who votes the officials to power and what right do these voters have to put the officials in power?

People talk about how a country as vast as ours cannot produce sporting champions. The answer is, firstly, a lack of sporting ethos, sport culture and the stranglehold of a few officials on the sport. Look around and you will find in every sport some officials who have made a career out of becoming officials. Yet Fazil Ahmed has the temerity to refer to one of India's greatest sportspersons as a paid coach. Well, Prakash could have been a paid coolie or a paid sweeper but he has done more for the sport than the honorary parasites that crowd Indian sport. Most

Prakash signing autographs.

of these honorary officials are leeches who suck the blood of sport and who, instead of serving the game, serve themselves by using the game.

Prakash's move has been welcomed not only by former players but by just about everybody who is keen on Indian sports. He now needs to quickly get to work by chalking out a calendar of events that will give maximum opportunity to the players to show their skills as also to see that the game gets a healthy injection of sponsorship. More importantly, he needs to see that he has with him others who are interested in the progress of sport and not for personal gain. And he should also show once he has got the federation firmly on the rails that he will not be like the others and cling to his chair. With the stature he has in the sport, he will always be consulted by those who follow him to the presidency of the federation. He has to watch out for the Trojan horses too, for make no mistake every effort will be made to try and scuttle the new organisation.

This is the time for all right-thinking people and true sports lovers to support Prakash as he embarks on the road that will set the tone to clean up Indian sports administration. Well done, Prakash and god be with you.

God certainly was on Mark Taylor's side as he batted to get back among the runs and saved not only his captaincy but his place in the side. Before the start of the first Test, just about everybody had given up hopes that Taylor would be able to get runs in the Test match again. Not only was he looking heavier but he was also making basic errors that a school boy is aware of. He was chasing deliveries well outside the off-stump and getting out caught. It was quite clear that in his anxiety to score runs, he was trying to play every ball and thus reaching out to even deliveries that he would have normally left alone. This is what happens to most batsmen who are having a bad patch for they think that the more they play, the quicker their bad patch will go.

In the second innings he played a lot straighter, left plenty of deliveries alone and went on to score a century. It was an innings that brought out the strong character he is and showed his mental toughness. It may not have saved Australia from defeat but it gave them the heart to rebound from it.

Greg Blewett likes the English bowling for he scored his third century in as many Tests against them. The failure of the Waugh Brothers in the first Test showed how crucial their contribution is to Australia's victories. Yet it is only a fool who will write off the Aussies. The England team does look a lot more positive and its body language was very aggressive in the first Test. But as can be seen with Mark Taylor's return to form, it takes just one innings to turn cricketing fortunes around and at the time of writing this piece, the Australians had struck back in the second Test. Whether they go on to win will be known by the time this is out and for the sake of a great Ashes series, I hope they do!

Just as I was about to finish this column, came another piece of good news—the appointment of Retired Chief Justice V.Y. Chandrachud as a one-man committee to enquire into the allegations of match fixing that has been making the news, for far too long have Indian cricketers been maligned by loose talk about their integrity. Not only the players but their families have been dragged into conversation at cocktail parties, casual gatherings and street corners by people who see a non-cricketing reason for everything that does not go according to expectations. We may not be champions at cricket, but we are champions at character assassination and it does not necessarily have to be the character of a cricketer. Retired Chief Justice Chandrachud has been given the power to call on anybody and that is good because it will settle once and for all the nasty stories that have besmirched the name of cricketers and Indian cricket. Well done, Cricket Control Board!

26.06.1997

*...d Ali, Indian
...e phenomenon
...he West Indies
...us Indian great
...oyd.*

AZHAR DESERVES CREDIT
for Abid Deed

It was good to see that determined, never-say-die cricketer Syed Abid Ali being given a purse at the Wankhede Stadium last week. Here was a cricketer who epitomised what hundred percent effort meant. With Abid in the side, the captain was guaranteed a player who would play selflessly and give it everything he got. Being part of the same team as Abid was an education because it was not just on the field but off the field that he was helpful to youngsters. I will never forget how at the Brabourne Stadium he once corrected me when I referred to a dark complexioned official of Mumbai cricket as 'the black gentleman' and was gently chided by Abid that black was wrong word and dark was the correct way to describe. Abid knew that I was not being disrespectful but was only trying to tell the others who the gentleman was, since they could not place a face to the name I had mentioned.

On the field, he was a dynamo particularly running between the wickets and though it often looked dangerous Abid was invariably home. On my Test debut in the West Indies, we suddenly lost three wickets for 70-odd after a good opening start and with 50 more runs remaining, the West Indians suddenly started to exert more pressure with some hostile bowling and brilliant fielding. Abid who had been promoted came up to me and said that we should look for quick singles, as that would rattle the West Indies. That is exactly what happened. Clive Lloyd was a fielder to whom you did not take a run if the ball was anywhere remotely close to him but Abid took that as a challenge and it was to Lloyd that we took most of our singles. Clive got so annoyed that he gave away overthrows trying to score a direct hit that took us nearer our target and before you knew it we were on the threshold of a famous victory. It was at this point that Abid's big heart was seen. We needed a boundary for a win but he took a single and gave me the strike saying that I deserved to hit the winning stroke and as Barret bowled the wrong one I shouted 'Googles' and pulled the ball one bounce into the boundary boards, Abid was next to me shouting '*Shabaash Bachha*, Congratulations!' I could not believe that playing in my first Test I had the honour of hitting the wining run but it was only because Abid gave me the strike. It was our first ever victory over West Indies in a Test match.

Sunil Gavaskar – shadow practising.

Funnily, a few months later India was on the verge of another famous victory and once again Abid was at the crease. This time, however, he hit the winning runs and there is the famous footage of Abid running back to get hold of one of the stumps as a souvenir while everyone else was running to the cover of the pavilion.

The Indian captain Mohammad Azharuddin took the initiative in organising this benefit game and he deserves compliments for showing concern for a former player. Not many may know about it but the captain invariably makes a personal contribution to the beneficiary and he does it without any fanfare or publicity. He and Sachin Tendulkar have rarely missed a benefit match even if it has meant travelling long distances by bus on some pretty ordinary roads. This is in stark contrast to some others who turn up especially if the matches are at major cities and stay in five star hotels, run up huge bills and then not even appear on the field or appear for an hour or so and then rush back to the room for whatever reason.

Abid, who has gone through a hard time, was lucky that there was time in the normally crowded schedule to have a match and that too with another international team but what about others like him who have chosen to stay abroad? Players like Rusi Surti, V. Subramanyam who live in Australia come readily to mind. Should their services to the game be forgotten just because they no longer live in India? What about Ramnath Parker? He is not in a position to ask for benefits, so should he be forgotten?

The Board does have a benevolent fund scheme but when you consider that till the early 1980s there were hardly any international matches, should there not be a fresh look at those who played before the rush of the Tests and internationals started and TV rights revenues started coming into the Board's coffers?

The time has come for the Board to ask each association that gets a Test and especially One-day internationals to set aside five percent for every ticket sold as well as five percent of the advertising revenue for a benefit fund for the players from its state. The way the cricket schedule is nowadays, there are few opportunities to have a benefit match and to organize one, takes a lot of time and effort. It would be simpler to set aside a sum from the gate and advertising revenue to be given to a player that the executive committee decides should get a benefit. Part of the fund can be kept aside to help out a player for any medical expenses.

Mumbai Cricket Association has taken the lead in many aspects of Indian cricket and it would be fitting if they took the lead in this as well. They do not have a game during the coming tour of Australia so they have the time to think and adopt a system that will help their cricketers without compromising on their dignity.

If one match like that organized for Abid makes us all feel so good, then what a well-organized system to assist other cricketers will make us feel? It is never too late. Start now.

05.02.1998

Clockwise:
...eat Ramakant
...Sri Lankan
...dust — Arjuna
...unga. Former
...wicketkeeper
...Mongia.

Sad Case of **RANATUNGA**

There were plenty of happy pictures of the victorious Indian team that returned from Sharjah and why not? They had achieved a truly memorable victory and after years of returning from Sharjah empty-handed, they had now returned with a trophy and some fantastic cricket memories for those who had followed their game.

But there was also one picture that saddened the heart and that was of Sri-Lankan captain, Arjuna Ranatunga, who had arrived in Mumbai and was trying to contact some friends on the phone. Why was that picture a sad one? It was because Ranatunga was on his way to Indore according to the caption under the photograph, to answer the summons issued to him by the court in relation to the case filed against him and Sachin Tendulkar for the abandonment of the One-day fixture in December. Sad, because a visiting captain should have to fly all the way from his home to a court in India to answer for a decision that was not even taken by him.

Ranatunga was not even at the crease when the match referee decided to call off the match because the pitch, in his opinion, was dangerous and unfit to play cricket. As captain of his team, Ranatunga was entirely justified in being concerned about the possibility of injuries to his players as was Tendulkar, who was the fielding side captain. He too knew that the pitch was hardly likely to improve and with more play, would have crumbled even more and his batsmen would also be in serious problems when they went in to bat. Whatever their reasoning, and whether it was hasty or wrong, the fact remains that the final decision was not theirs and so to be hauled before a court of law is a little too harsh.

Hopefully, the court will understand; otherwise captains and even other players will be open to litigation from all quarters. For example, there could be litigation as to why the captain chose to bat or field, why he sent a particular player to open the batting or why he made a fielding change or a bowling replacement. The batsmen may have to answer in court why he played a particular stroke or a bowler may have to defend why he bowled that particular delivery. The umpires may also be open to litigation on the decision they give and who knows the selectors may be next and the cricket control boards and then the ICC may also be the ones defending every single action in court. It just wouldn't stop, and cricketers and administrators will make more appearance in court than on field, giving rise to a new breed of statisticians who will be recording the number of times a player or administrator was present in the court. Who in his right senses would want to captain his country if at the end of the day he has to go before the court and explain the reason for every action of his? Ranatunga was by himself and there was no information that his board was helping him with his legal defence. Perhaps the players should now insist on a clause in their contracts that if they are hauled before a court of law for their action on the field then the boards should look after the legal costs. It may not come to that for the court may well throw the case out and which will definitely discourage others from pressing for such litigation but still, the time has come for the boards to make sure that the conditions for the sale of tickets are clearly defined and no legal hassles are made for the players who are in no way connected to the sale of the tickets. The players do not get a share of the tickets sale and so should not be party to litigation brought upon the controlling body or its affiliated units for whatever reason.

Speaking of sharing, one is not sure whether the Indian cricket team shares the fines imposed on its players by the ICC match referees or whether it is the offending player himself who bears the entire brunt. When I was the manager of the Indian team for a couple of matches and Mongia was fined, it was a surprise to know that he was to pay the fine himself and the team was not going to contribute. This is in contrast to when a player wins a cash award, for then everybody wants to be given a share in it; even if it's a cash award that is spontaneously announced by an individual or firm and not one of the pre-announced awards before the match or tournament begins. The best way to generate team spirit is not only to share in the joy of winning but also to be able to be a part of the losing side and share the blame equally rather than point fingers at each other.

The saying that sorrow follows great joy could be seen in the passing away of Ramakant Desai so soon after the Sharjah victory. Ramakant was only 58 years old but had been unwell for sometime which is why he resigned as the chairman of the selection committee only a couple of months back. The cricket board must be thankful that it accepted his resignation and thus did not have his death on its hands for there was a school of thought that Ramakant should continue as chairman even if he could not attend the meetings.

The tributes that have come from all over India have one common theme and that was, that Ramakant was a gentleman through and through. Today, Sachin

Tendulkar has hordes of children following him wherever he goes but before the little champion there was Ramakant and I have said this often that he was like the 'Pied Piper' with little kids following him with an awestruck expression. He, along with Baloo Gupte and the late Vijay Manjrekar, was the one who made life a great deal comfortable when I first entered the Mumbai Ranaji Trophy team and later on, there was Ajit Wadekar and Dilip Sardesai who were of immense help. It is the guidance that one receives in one's formative years that is so important and I was fortunate to have Ramakant in the dressing room to help me overcome my nervousness.

To all of us and especially to the cricket loving public of Mumbai, he was simply 'Ramakant' and not 'Ramakant Desai'. Indian cricket has lost one of its top cricketers and I have lost not only a friend and a guide, but a hero as well! R.I.P Ramakant.

30.04.1998

OFFICIALS NEED
Red and Yellow Cards Too

There is not the slightest doubt that the eyes of the sporting world will be focused on the Football World Cup over the next few weeks. It is without question the most popular sport in the world. It is inexpensive and can be played anywhere and there are more rags to riches stories in football than in any other sport. In South America it is as much a passion as cricket is in India, perhaps even more so and I remember asking Steve Bucknor who is also an international football referee besides being an international cricket umpire whether the passion for football in South America is greater than the passion for cricket in India. His reply 'they kill for football down there' was enough of an answer and the Columbian football team would readily second that opinion.

Well, they almost killed each other for the top job in football, didn't they? 'Sepp' Blatter and Lennart Johansson who were contesting for the job of the chief of FIFA have gone on record as having not only travelled the world to canvas for votes but also spent over 1.1 million dollars in doing so. Blatter, who announced his candidature for the presidency of FIFA only a few months ago, has spent over $ 3,00,000 while Johansson has spent over $ 8,00,000. Blatter being the secretary was helped in his expenses by friends, and UEFA spent the money for Johansson as he lobbied for votes to succeed Joe Havelange as the FIFA president. Now the FIFA president's job is honorary and part time, so to spend the kind of money Blatter and Johansson have done, does raise the eyebrow more than a bit. Sure it is a position of enormous power and influence, still to spend over a million dollars does leave room for doubt that the position does allow a possibility of recouping the expense. Of course for a truly wealthy person such expense might be peanuts and the position gives a high profile and recognition in any part of the world which his wealth and business would hardly give and thus one can understand the eagerness to be in the top job. After all one can meet presidents, prime ministers and other celebrities and even be photographed with them and be seen on TV. No wonder there is a scramble for such honorary position and once in power, it can get so intoxicating that ways and means are devised to stay in power permanently. Havelange was the president for twenty-four years and that is perhaps three to four times the career span of the average footballer and hey, there are no yellow cards or red cards either!

I.S. Bindra

It is just a nice cushy globe-trotting job with no accountability. That is what should be the first item on the agenda of the Sports Minister as the Central government starts to look to formulate a sports policy. It is a bit too late to help with the Sydney Olympics in the year 2000 but if a national sports committee is formed consisting of eminent sports personalities, media persons and some administrators, it would go a long way in helping Indian sports. The Committee should be limited to no more than fifteen people at the most, though even that seems a number which will encourage more argument than proper discussion not to mention politics which is there in every sport in every country in the world.

But the aim should be to cut down on talk and get men of action in national sports committee. From among sportspersons, one can immediately think of greats like Milkha Singh, Ramanathan Krishnan, Prakash Padukone, Kapil Dev, Michael Ferreira, Dr. Vece Paes to name a few, and from the administrators one can name Mr. Dalmiya, Mr M.A.M. Ramaswamy, Mr.Bindra who was also the president of Table Tennis Federation of India apart from being the President of Board of Control for Cricket in India. Once again there are a few names that crop up immediately when one thinks of administrators who have made a substantial and positive contribution to sport. Similarly, from the world of media, people of dynamism and a love for sport like Khalid Ansari, Aveek Sarkar, M.J. Akbar, Vinod Mehta again naming just a few that come to mind instantly. They may not be covering sports but they have in the past, and today know what management is about, they are in a position where they are above the politics that rules sports and as such in sports media too. Form a committee with men like that and make them the final authority and see how our sport will progress.

Leaving it in the hands of honorary servants of the game has hardly worked in the first fifty years of our Independence. Why not, therefore, take a new initiative and chart new territory and give the committee a few years to show results? But, of course, the crucial part is whether the Sports Minister is serious about the development of sports or whether the move to inculcate a new sports policy is going to mean the same old wine in a new bottle. We shall know soon enough whether the old power brokers who have run Indian sports are still pulling the strings or whether the new government has a will of its own and is prepared to look at new ideas and new ways to develop and make Indian sports into a world-class phenomenon. We shall soon know whether it is only lip service or whether a real service is going to be done to Indian sports. The time cannot be more ideal, for the country is running emotionally high after the achievements last month and there is a new enthusiasm and renewed hope in the future of India. One has seen how sporting triumph lifts the country up e.g. Sharjah in April and how sporting disaster like World Cup Hockey in Utrecht can demoralize the country. Sporting triumphs indicate that the youth of the country are full of vigor, energy and strength and it gives hope to the upcoming generation wanting to emulate their sporting heroes. Question is whether the tired old men who make the decisions on Indian sport are prepared to let the young dynamic India take over? That would be real sporting of them!

11.06.1998

*... playing another
... Play resume
... Christchurch
... during the New
... tour*

Some **DRESS SENSE**, Please!

Did you know that you do not have to be an India player to get the India shirt and India cap? All you have to be is a pretty face and give the Indian player a smile and maybe an idea or two by acting coy and you will get the Indian shirt off him in a jiffy. He will then conveniently forget that the shirt has been given to him by the Board of Control for Cricket in India (BCCI) because he is deemed to be good enough out of the millions to be in the squad of fourteen or sixteen to represent India in international matches. He has got there by dint of hard work and when he first gets his cap and his India shirts, he will even wear it to bed at night and not want to part with it. But then he plays for a few years, becomes popular and rich and the importance of the cap and the India shirt begins to wear thin. What the heck! He gets a cap for every tour, why, sometimes his sponsor makes an India cap for him. The Cricket Control Board does not say a word to him for not wearing the standard issue cap for all the team members tour, and every series he has more India caps than he wants. Ditto with the shirts. He has more India shirts again courtesy the Cricket Control Board and his sponsor, than he can wear in a lifetime. Oh yes, then there are the shirts for the One-day games. You know how many One-day tournaments the Indian team plays. So, for every tournament he gets shirts which are of different designs. Where is he going to keep all this and especially while returning from an overseas tour, what with all the shopping and the freebies that he has got. What better way to make place for the shopping to be accommodated in the suitcase than by giving away an India shirt or two to a pretty face? Who knows he may get more than a smile from the pretty face!

What a pity the India shirt and cap mean so little to some of the members of the Indian team. An even greater pity is that the shirts that were seen on the backs of the cheer leaders of a liquor group in Christchurch belonged to players who one thought were really proud to be playing for India and were among the few in the current team who were pained at the effort level of the rest of the team and were among the success stories of the current New Zealand tour. These players gave more than one hundred percent on the field and were really hurt when India could not level the Test series and win the One-day series. That's why it is even more

The late Vijay Manjrekar.

amazing that they gave off the shirts that they wore with such courage, dignity and fortitude to a bunch of girls who did nothing but jump up and down, mostly at the wrong time and generally looked absurd at the game. Was it disappointment that the rest of their team mates did not do enough that made them give away their shirts or was it sheer 'couldn't care less we get these shirts every other day' attitude that made them take it off?

The Indian Cricket Board does not allow merchandising of its shirts and quite rightly so. It is only players who play for India who should be wearing the national colour and so they cannot be bought off a stall at the ground or at a sports shop. Perhaps that is not entirely true, for today the India shirt along with the sponsors logo is available at sports shops in Mumbai and the Board does not even know about it. The principle behind not making the cap or the shirt available to all and sundry is simply because the India colours are sacred and they have to be earned and not purchased. There has to be a copyright on the colours, the logo of the Indian team. Not only that, the Board must put down a clause in the players' contract that they will not give away any of the equipment that the Board gives them without the written permission of the Board president. Sure one can exchange caps or shirts with the opposition players for one is sure that they will be kept as souveneir at home and not worn. Even giving a cap or a shirt for a charity is fine so long as it is genuine charity and approved by the Board.

There has to be a certain pride in wearing the India colours and preserving it. The late Vijay Manjrekar once forced an official to remove the India tie he was wearing because he had not played for India. Unfortunately, they don't make players like him any more, for how else can one explain the physio and the doctor of the team being allowed to wear the India cap by the current players? They simply don't care and that lack of pride in the colours shows in their performances. So you do not have to have cricketing talent to get the India cap and shirt. You could be a pretty face and the India colours could be yours, baby!

22.01.1999

...re:
...ars of Indian
...Farokh Engineer,
...ir Ali Bose and
...r Ali Khan
...n; Mumbai's
...ket stadium.

Visiting My Hero, **JAISIMHA**

He looked like a baby who was fast asleep. There was congestion in the bronchial area which made him occasionally take a deeper breath but apart from that there was absolutely no sign that he had a few hours left. It was with great trepidation that I had entered the house for the one image I did not want to be left with was of my hero suffering. That was the reason I had been reluctant to visit him after my return from England. I wanted to remember the dashing debonair, ever smiling person and was afraid of what I would see if I called on him. His lovely wife Junie playfully called me 'darpok' but it was true. I was being a coward and selfish for I wanted to retain only the happy images. It was as always the wife who put it into the proper perspective. No wonder they are called the better halves. Pammi said that he has been fond of you for so long, so even if he sees you for five seconds he will feel a little better and the pain he is having will ease for a few seconds.

Unfortunately, my flight the previous day had got delayed by over four hours so I could not go but I did the next day and I am glad that I did. My hero looked the same as he always did. Fortunately, the illness that ravages the body had left his handsome face untouched. There were no gaunt cheeks, no sunken eyes and as I wrote in the beginning, he looked like a baby who was sleeping. I held his hand, stroked it willing him silently to get up and address me by the name he always called me. Gaavuskar...! He never called me by my first name. May be when he was talking about me to others but he always called me by my last name and it was the most correct pronunciation of the name ever. Nobody, not even my family, has made our surname so good as my hero did.

My first glimpse of my hero was at Brabourne stadium when the Indian team had come to practise and the image of the players laughing and joking as they made their way to the nets is something I'll never forget. To a player who has just started playing for his school, it gave the impression that there was so much fun and enjoyment in playing the game even at the highest level.

That era was truly the romantic era of Indian cricket. What good looking guys we had playing for India and what an entertaining and dashing game they played! There was Mansur Ali Khan Pataudi with his cap drawn over his bad right eye, there was the lazy elegance of Salim Durani, there was the handsome Abbas Ali Baig, there was the dare devil batting and wicket keeping of Farokh Engineer and Budhi Kunderan and the greatest excitement they brought to the game whether in front of the stumps or behind it. And there was my hero, collar turned up and a silk kerchief knotted around the neck and the shirt fluttering in the breeze. On anybody else this would have made them look like 'mawaalis' but these guys looked like cricketers, walked like cricketers and whenever we overheard them, they talked like cricketers. We heard so many stories of the way they lived life after playing hours were over and this combined with the way they played cricket made us want to take up the game even more.

It was my good fortune that on my first overseas tour he was in the team as well. There were many hours that I spent speaking with him, or rather listening to him, and it was a great learning experience. In those days, the hotels had rooms which were really huge and not the matchbox-style rooms that are in vogue today and so, most of the players would gather in one room, mostly Ajit Wadekar's and the topic would invariably be – cricket be it the day's play or what to do the next day. These were informal team meetings and not those that were compulsory to attend. Yet just about every member would be there and because it was a free-wheeling discussion even a newcomer like me could put in my two paisa bit now and again.

It turned out to be a dream debut tour for me but even as I returned to India, the one thought that was overriding was that even if I had got half the runs I would have been happy so long as the remaining half went to my hero and the other gem of a person – Salim Durani. For then they too would have been termed as having had a good tour and would have been selected to tour England a month later. That was not to be and though I played with 'Salim uncle' later, I never again got the chance to play in the same team as my hero. Of course we met several times later and had some great evenings together with my hero as usual being the centre of attraction.

I have never been envious or jealous of anybody so far in my life but I am jealous of God Almighty who now has my hero for company but even he does not know what he is in for. For make no mistake the angels are all going to be charmed by my hero and he will only watch helplessly as we did here on mother earth.

Motganhalli Laxminarsu Jaisimha born on 3 March 1939, reclaimed by God on 7 July 1999.

My hero. Always! And forever!

08.07.1999

Motganhalli Laxminarsu Jaisimha
1939-1999

EVERYBODY HURTS...

One of the occupational hazards of a sporting career is injuries. There has hardly ever been a sportsperson who has played at the top level for some years who has not suffered from an injury. It could well be an injury which is minor and which has made him miss the odd international event and not necessarily a serious one that puts him out of sporting circulation for a few months. Sometimes it may be an injury that has not occurred at the competition but could well be at home when he/she is trying to do some household chores or at the office or club and again here it does not have to be playing the sport he/she is proficient at. More than the physical recovery aspect, it is the psychological recovery from the fear of the injury that takes longer and can actually have a major setback to a sporting career.

The Monica Seles' stabbing incident is fresh in one's mind where though the physical recovery was in the normal course of time, the psychological recovery has not really taken place. Seles was the commanding no. 1 in women's tennis when she was stabbed in the back by a person who described himself as a Steffi Graf fan and wanted to see Graf back as no.1. Graf herself would have preferred to get back her no. 1 ranking through deeds on the court and though Seles came back to tennis, it was after two years during which she underwent psychological restructuring. She remains a dangerous opponent, that aura of invincibility around her was gone forever and she looked frightened on the court during her first matches on her comeback and seemed to be constantly looking over her shoulder for another madman to attack her. The Seles – Graf rivalry on court had made women's tennis a very attractive proposition for tennis promoters and with one stab it all went to zero.

There have been fatalities too. Ayrton Senna's car crashed while coming off a turn and he died leaving the motor racing sport the poorer for he was admired by all including his fellow participants, and in the cut throat business of Grand Prix racing that itself is an achievement. Today Michael Schumacher is out of action after he was lucky to survive a crash and though the marvels of modern medicine and surgical practices will mean he will be back on track sooner than a similar injury a decade or so ago, there will be tremendous interest to see how he copes with it psychologically.

Nari Contractor, executing a shot.

Boxing too has seen some serious damage being done to some and Mohammad Ali, the Greatest, is an example. Though he was seriously injured only once when his jaw was broken, it is the blows that he took during his career that has led to his current situation where he is suffering from Parkinson's disease and is but a pale shadow of the athlete that the world followed and many loved to hate.

Physical contact sport always has the risk of a player getting injured quite seriously and rugby, American Rules Football and even soccer and hockey are sports which have seen some serious injuries which have cut short budding and promising careers and has left the sport the poorer for it.

In the world of cricket too there have been some horrible injuries. Who can forget the blow to Nari Contractor that almost killed him? Though the gutsy Contractor came back to the game, the selectors did not want to take a chance and did not pick him for Tests again. Those were, of course, the pre-helmet days where a batsman relied on his eye to get out of the line of the screaming bouncers. There were plenty of broken fingers then because the equipment used was not as good as it is now. The injuries that players suffer are mainly muscular and one of the reasons is that minor injures are carried into the next game simply because there is no time for rest and recovery and the minor injury then becomes a major one. The competition for places is intense and no player wants to miss out due to an injury and let his competitor take his place.

The little champion, Sachin Tendulkar of course has no such fears of a competitor taking his place. His back injury has caused immense concern to millions of his admirers who are keeping their fingers crossed not just for a speedy recovery but a complete recovery. He still has a good ten years of plundering runs ahead of him and it is important that rather than look at a short term he should be looking to his future and get the correct diagnosis and then take proper measures to see that it does not recur. The injury first flared up in Chennai which is hot and humid right through the year and again in Colombo which has similar weather. At the moment of writing, he is likely to play in Singapore but to do so after the pain he had during his century knock may not be a wise thing. Of course, he alone knows the pain and how much he can bear and there is no doubting his fierce commitment to Indian cricket. Still the feeling generally is that he should get investigations done where his back is monitored twenty-four hours if necessary to see if there are certain types of movement that bring the spasm on. He may be the captain of India and the best batsman in the world but he is still a little kid who wants to play all the time, and those close to him must make him understand that his problematic back needs proper treatment and corrective therapy. He is a national treasure and such treasurers are rare in India.

So little champion, take care of your back so that you can continue to bring glory to the country for a long, long time!

02.09.1999

WELCOME Aboard, Refs!

One of the smartest moves by the ICC in the early 1990s was to set up the position of the ICC match referee. The ICC was worried about the fall in the standards of behaviour of the players towards the umpires and wanted to ensure that it did not deteriorate to the levels of baseball in America where it is common to see players and umpires almost coming to blows even as they are eyeball to eyeball breathing each other's carbondioxide. In ice hockey, players get into a scuffle very easily and the umpire has to wait for a break in the scuffle to intervene and pull the players away from each other.

The presence of the ICC match referee has indeed helped, for with players getting fined and even suspended for showing the slightest disagreement with the umpire's decision, the players have to keep their emotions in check at least till they get into the privacy of the dressing rooms where all hell can be let loose and often is. The game is better off for it, for arguing with an umpire's decision however horrible and wrong it can be is not a good sight and is a poor example for budding cricketers watching on TV. Ask me, when I watched the replay of my disappointment over the leg before decision in Melbourne, Australia, in 1980-1981, I was ashamed of myself. The walkout that followed was not because of the umpiring decision but because of the comment passed by a couple of Australian fielders when I was on my way to the pavilion. It just added fuel to the fire and made me go over the top and ask my partner to walk off. Fortunately, the manager of the team ensured that Chetan Chauhan did not cross the boundary line but stayed inside it and so the match continued. But for those remarks made by the Australian players, I would have carried on to the dressing room and given vent to my anger over there, but the provocation was not the decision itself but the remarks by the players and this is where the ICC, especially the match referees, are not doing justice.

We have seen how remarks by players against each other led to the clash between Raman Lamba and Rashid Patel which not only brought Indian cricket but the game into disrepute, and Lamba and Patel were suspended from playing cricket for a year. The way things are going on in international cricket today the situation is ripe for another showdown, unless ICC referees wake up and start taking action

Glen McGrath giving a mouthful to West Indian, Ramnaresh Sarwan.

and provide protection to players from other players, just as umpires are being protected today by the threat of fines and suspension if players show any dissent at their decisions.

In recent times, the behaviour of the New Zealand players on the field has been boorish, to say the least. Not only did the Indians get an earful when they toured New Zealand but even here in India the Kiwis are up to mouthing abuse at the Indian batsmen. They have been doing so because they have found no match referee with the courage to reprimand them and so we saw in England during the World Cup the sledging that went on at Ridley Jacobs in the match New Zealand lost against the West Indies. Jacobs had the last laugh of course playing a match winning innings on a difficult pitch but that is not the point. Then in the series against England, New Zealand went on and on against the English batsmen and it did not make for pleasant viewing. People who are snarling hardly ever make a good-looking picture and just sends the wrong signals to everybody that is excepting the match referee who seems to think his job is only to protect the umpire from bad behaviour from the players.

Unfortunately, players who are the recipients of the abuse feel that they will be less than manly if they complain and one suspects that even the match referees feel the same way, and that's why the reluctance to take action which is not bringing any glory to the game but giving a wrong example to kids watching at the ground or on TV. Sledging to my mind is showing dissent, not at the umpire but at the opposition player and that needs to be stopped forthwith. There is the example of Glen McGrath who was fined heavily for his verbals and now is seldom if ever seen resorting to it and surprise, surprise, he is still taking plenty of wickets and winning matches for Australia. So sledging is not needed to fire up anybody to perform at his best.

Not only New Zealand players but even a New Zealand umpire had gone over the top recently and abused a TV commentator in Sharjah. Those who saw the match on TV will recall the controversial decision given to rule Aravinda de Silva out in the finals. The ball had bounced off Inzamam-ul Haq's hands and hit the ground and then lodged between his thighs. The third umpire Steve Dunne ruled Aravinda out because he held the view that the ball had hit Inzamam's trouser cuff and thus technically not hit the ground. The commentators Jonathan Agnew and Rameez Raja felt that since the third umpire seemed to be taking his time to arrive at a decision, there was enough doubt and the benefit of the doubt should go to the batsman. Reacting to their comments, Steve Dunne came up to the commentary box and in full hearing of the others in the VIP boxes, used foul language against Agnew who was only describing what he saw. One does not know if Dunne later apologised, but his behaviour that day should be severely condemned and ICC would be failing in its duty if they do not remove him from the panel.

The time has come to banish the bullies from the game as we enter the new millennium. Will the ICC do it?

Your guess is as good as mine.

28.10.1999

Match fixing tainted late South African skipper Hansie Cronje.

Waiting for **THE DUST TO CLEAR**

One thing that strikes you immediately on arriving in England is that the sport that is loved more than any other is football and the talking point is whether England would qualify for the knock-out stages of Euro 2000. In the event, Romania outplayed them and dashed the hopes of the football-mad fans. For the next few weeks, the media will be full of post mortems and the recrimination, that this should have been done and that should have been done, columns will be frequent along with the calls to sack Kevin Keegan and Co.

It makes for a change in reading from what is appearing on the front pages of Indian papers, for if football is the big sport in England then cricket is the number one sport in India though it does look that it will slip down the ladder considerably the way things are going at the moment. Cricket and cricketers are not exactly the flavour of the month nowadays and are being rubbished by anybody and everybody and by even those who have a faint acquaintance with the game. This is sad, for as the unfolding Hansie Cronje drama is showing us that, by and large, the rest of the South African cricketers were clean and above board and that may well be the case in India too where there may be the odd bad apple but the great majority of the cricketers would be people to be proud of. To paint them all with the same tar is not fair. What is even more unfair is to try and make your own name and reputation by spoiling someone else's hard-earned one through innuendo and unsubstantiated and vague allegations. Cricketers are human with failings, which are probably common, and they hurt as well when something ill is spoken about them. That's why one hopes when all the dust is clear and the inquiries complete, there will be the bigness of heart to accept that allegations made against some were wrong and amends made for it.

But onto pleasanter subjects and nothing can be more pleasant than trying to help raise funds for a worthy cause. I have been playing for the last few years just one game of cricket and that is for a charity called Wellbeing. The game is invariably around the same time as the Lord's Test and Wimbledon Tennis so it is the ideal time to be in England as one can get to see a bit of both. Sir David Frost is one of the organisers and the match is played at Sir Victor Blank's ground in Chippinghurst just outside London. The participants are leading industrialists and businessmen from England along with former players like, yours truly.

Sometime the managers and a couple of members of the team touring England also come and play. The companies of the industrialists and the businessmen make a hefty donation to the charity and there is also an auction of memorabilia between innings where a lot of money is raised. It is a family outing, for children can keep themselves occupied with the games and rides that are just next to the ground and there is free ice cream and candy going for them as well as painters to paint their faces. So everybody has a good time and plenty of funds are raised for the charity.

It was this game which gave the incentive to do something similar in

Hansie confessing his guilt.

India and so for the CHAMPS Foundation the idea was used after modifying it slightly. The match in England is a 35 overs a side contest but for CHAMPS it was decided to have double wicket competition with a leading Indian industrialist teaming with a member of the 1983 World Cup winning side members. It was again a most enjoyable day and a good amount was raised and even simple ordinary folk contributed and that was the most heartening of all. CHAMPS was looking to have the second fixture in February but the ground was given for the South Africa vs Board President's game and moreover, since not too many names have come up for the recognition that the foundation wants to give, the trustees felt that it was okay to postpone the game. CHAMPS is the acronym for caring, helping, assisting, motivating and promoting sports persons from any field of sport who need assistance. Do let us know, if you have any suggestions. As a rule, sportspersons are not going to ask for assistance, for they have too much pride and self respect to spread their hands and that's why CHAMPS assistance to them is termed recognition of their contribution to sport. The foundation has been fortunate to get some of the biggest names in Indian industry and business to support it and it is looking forward to sports lovers to suggest ways and means to improve and to recognise sportspersons who may have fallen on hard times.

As for the match that is to be played around the time you are reading this I am hoping to get to a half century for a player has to retire after getting to a fifty. In all these years I have not managed to get there and for three consecutive years, I got out for 18. The bowling has not been all that bad. I have regularly picked wickets with the new ball and then bowling my 'mixed bhajiyas'. But that is not good enough for I must get that half century and am hoping that the new millennium will be the year when I get there.

23.06.2000

...a Indian premiere
...c championship
...: Deodhar Trophy
...nji Trophy.

GIVE MORE, Take Less!

The lull from international cricket will hopefully give domestic cricket a chance to be in the forefront again. For far too long domestic cricket has been neglected with the number of international matches being played hogging the limelight. The biggest blow has been the absence of the India regulars' participation in domestic cricket, for that does not then help reflect an accurate picture of the ability of the domestic performers. Now that there's a gap till the Australians come over, it will be interesting to see how many Indian stars participate in the domestic tournaments. Of course nobody will just pull out saying they need rest but may do so on the pretext of being injured, and while having a break and a rest is no bad thing so long as it is just that, it must be ensured that the break days or rest days are not utilised by the players in doing commercials. This is where the Board will have to be very strict and ensure that if a star is not playing because of 'injury', then he is not doing anything else commercially during that time but doing everything to ensure quick recovery from the injury. Surely if a player is going to miss a Ranji game saying he is unwell or injured and is doing an advertisement film for a soft drink, scooter, bank or whatever at the same time, then he needs to be disciplined and made to understand that all the commercials he is doing is because he started with domestic cricket and if he is going to turn his back on that then Indian cricket will also turn its back on him. Of course this is more fantasy than reality for we know that when it comes to taking action, then all the politics of the Board cames into play.

It is a real pity that domestic cricket does not get its due. It is sad to hear of venues where there are no proper toilets in the players' dressing rooms, where umpires do not have a proper changing room and where water is carried in a plastic bucket and offered to the players in dirty plastic cups at the drinks interval. Apart from a few major centres, no other centre wants to hold domestic cricket for there are no profits in this but only hard work and don't forget the officials are all honourary; so they are not expected to work hard but only be there for the perks of international matches. That, after all, is their reward for serving Indian cricket though the apt motto would be 'Those who serve themselves first serve the game as well'.

Gavaskar and his West Zone team mates holding the Duleep Trophy.

We are prepared to spend money on consultancies so we have today more than one cricket consultant from overseas. They may well make a contribution but what is important is the pitches and playing conditions and those are not being looked at. The pitches committee could do with some help from an expert from overseas who could come down, have a look at our soil and offer advice on how to make our pitches hard and bouncy, but that is not the glamour aspect, for groundsmen do not use management jargon that impresses and so the most important part of our cricket, the grounds and pitches get neglected. You can bring a hundred coaches and consultants and nothing will improve unless the ground conditions are attended to first. Right from the junior level to the first class level we have to give good surfaces to play on and a good outfield for the basics to be properly learnt and developed. Every single association gets a share of the revenue from the Board of Control for Cricket in India (BCCI). Yet how many of them use it to promote the game and develop the infrastructure? Invariably the funds lie in a bank or in some official's company as a deposit, and the game and the players get nothing and because they have a vote, the Board is reluctant to take action against these associations.

It would be truly interesting to see what all these consultants of Board are going to do about the above problems. All that is likely to happen is that a good chunk of money will go to these consultants who will use some jargon to show that they have done their bit and laugh all the way to the bank. You and I, the ordinary cricket lovers, will tear our hair out in frustration, for nothing will change.

Bringing in outsiders for an impartial, different perspective is no bad thing. All major companies do that when they are looking to expand and restructure but the Board has shown reluctance to change, falling back on the excuse of the Constitution, which is the reason why yours truly has been saying for so long that it is the articles of association and constitution of the sporting bodies, national as well as state and district levels, that need to be looked at and amended if necessary if Indian sport is to move forward. But who has the will to do it? Nobody, not even the government, for if you have noticed that the Board has conveniently ignored the CBI's observations against it while at the same time accepting those against the players. The Board has shown thus that it does not give a damn about anybody, so who are you and me to complain?

Have a Happy X-mas and a better New Year than the last one.

21.12.2000

..xman, Olympic,
..ce – Karnam
...r; Indian
...in are – Pullela
...d; and All-
...Champion Peter

GOPI Showed His Bottle

What a week this has been for the lads from Andhra Pradesh! First Pullela Gopichand becomes only the second Indian to win the All England Badminton Championship and then a couple of days later, V.V.S. Laxman becomes the highest scorer in Tests for an Indian in an innings and in a partnership with Rahul Dravid gave India the chance of a victory to level the series one all and stop Australia's winning streak. Gopichand's victory was truly terrific for from the first round he had to play a top class opponent and he beat them all without conceding a game. In an interview just before he left, he had said that the previous year he had been entering the quarter finals regularly and so this year he was hoping to do one better and get into the semis of all the events he participated in. Well, he went two better and not only entered the finals but also won the prestigious title. Like his mentor the great Prakash Padukone, Gopichand also is soft-spoken, modest and self-effacing, all qualities which are great off court but which can sometimes come in the way of delivering the knock-out punch on the court.

In this championship, Gopi was hardly stretched excepting in the semi-finals against the top seed and former All-England Champion Peter Grade. Watching it on TV one could see how Gopi was outmanoeuvering him and catching him on the wrong foot. Then when the scores became level at 13 all in the first game, doubts began to creep in. Is Gopi tired? Is he going to cave in now? But he showed he was made of sterner stuff by winning that game on extra points and then running away to a big lead in the second. In the second game, when he got a palpably wrong line call when he was leading 12-4, I was up screaming, raving and ranting at the gall of these people to point fingers at our officials and linesmen when theirs were so bad. Gopi seemed to have lost his concentration after that for it should have been 13-4 and it did appear that his mind was not quite on the task for the next few points quickly went to Gade. Then Gopi pulled himself up and finished off the match in style.

Since I was to catch a flight around the time the finals were to be played the next day I wasn't able to watch it live. On landing in Mumbai one inquired the score and in this cricket-mad country one got only the cricket scores when here was our countryman playing in the finals of a major badminton championship. No wonder

Prakash Padukone and Pullela Gopichand at a function.

other sportspersons complain that their sports get little recognition. On reaching home, one found that the national channel and not sports channel was showing the finals albeit a recorded version and though that meant Gopi had won, pure superstition made one not want to ask if he had. A quarter of an hour later when Gopi ran sideways and back toward the baseline to see the shuttle falling out and then raise his hands skywards, yours truly too did that.

Though one's cricket-playing days were over more than a decade ago, I truly cannot remember a moment that gave me so much elation as that moment when the shuttle fell out and we had a new champion. Yes, the victories in 1971, the 1979 one against Pakistan and the World Cup 1983 and World Championship victories are all moments that give gooseflesh but this one just beats them all and on a lighter note between watching Aishwarya Rai in a commercial and Gopichand doing the arm raising act, one would opt for the latter with not the slightest disrespect intended to the delightful former Miss World.

Karnam Malleswari winning the bronze medal in weightlifting at the Sydney Olympics earned kudos from all sports-loving Indians. She was also promised huge sums of money and though one does not know whether she has received the lot, it is now time for corporate and other bodies to come forward and reward Gopichand likewise. In fact Gopi has won a major and without wishing to compare different sports, he deserves as much if not more accolades and rewards.

This is also an ideal opportunity for the Badminton Association to vigorously market the game and capitalise on Gopichand's victory, for all advertising and marketing budgets will be in their infancy and the game can develop with the influx of capital so that the infrastructure also will get better.

Gopichand's victory is also a tribute to Prakash Padukone for it was at the Academy that he set up that Gopi began to believe in himself and went on from strength to strength as Aparna Popat is doing. The training the players receive there is raising the badminton standards in the country and Gopi's victory will be a huge incentive to all the youngsters at the Academy as well as the rest of the country.

The other Andhra boy, V.V.S. Laxman's problem seems to have been a lack of faith in his ability. Now that he has gone on to become Indian cricket's highest individual scorer in Tests, he will hopefully go on from strength to strength. The beauty of his knock was it came when India were down in the dumps and staring at defeat. His strokeful innings not only ensured that defeat was avoided but it also gave India a healthy bank of runs from where they could pressurise the Australians, and show that the World Champions too are only human and feel the tension and pressure like anybody else.

Yes, it truly was a wonderful sporting week for India and it was in the main due to two soft-spoken modest players from Andhra Pradesh.

15.03.2001

*Above:
r New York mayor
Guilliani; The
bus; The road
on in Mumbai.*

RASH DRIVING and Sad Exits

The deaths in a road accident of five budding chess champions has cast a pall of gloom over the chess-playing fraternity. It just seems such a senseless way to die and unless something is done on an urgent basis about our road manners, we are going to have more such horrific accidents where totally innocent people will die and families will be in mourning. Road accidents are there in every part of the world but the fatalities due to them is one of the highest in India and more people are killed in road accidents in our country than due to some major illnesses. What is even more galling is that the cause of the accidents are invariably 'professional' drivers. By professional I mean those who earn their living by driving a vehicle. If statistics were available, one would find that in most of the accidents it is the professional driver who is at fault. One just has to stand at a busy street in any city in India and observe how traffic laws are broken and one will find that invariably it is the professional driver who does so. Perhaps they have became blasé about their jobs, perhaps it is just the thrill of breaking a law, perhaps they don't give a damn about the law but more than all these, perhaps it is the sheer certainty that they will get away without even a slap on the wrist is what makes them do so.

Mumbai is the one city in India where traffic laws are observed more than anywhere else. But even here if the professional drivers find that there are no cops around, they will break the laws. The worst offenders are the drivers of the BEST buses. In all these years, one has yet to see a bus driver being stopped by a cop for infringing the traffic laws. This particular species is in a class of its own. A good-looking car is like a red rag to them and if not hitting it, they will try their utmost to scrap it. When they see ladies or elders trying to run to the bus stop, they will deliberately park the bus farther away from the stop and just as elder is reaching huffing and puffing to the stop they will take off even when there are plenty of seats available in the bus. There have been plenty of good Samaritan stories of bus conductors returning bags containing valuables and fortunes but hardly any of their colleague sitting in that cubical with that lethal weapon, the steering wheel.

Perhaps the real culprits are the driving schools whose only aim seems to churn out people who know how to put the vehicle in gear, and where the accelerator and brakes are. All the other requirements like observing signals and giving signals are not even taught except in some schools. If this is not done the worst lapse is in not teaching how to read road signs. If only there was strictness in giving licenses to motor training schools then we would have better drivers, but motor training schools sprout faster than mosquitoes, is an absolutely true Sidhuism.

If only there was more fear of law then there would be more observing of the traffic rules. I remember reading sometime ago how New York's mayor Rudy Guilliani tackled the crime situation in the city known as the crime capital of the world. He started by being strict with traffic offenders, for with the police department stretched to the limit trying to combat serious crime, traffic offenders got away. By targeting traffic violations, Guilliani sent the message that if small violation didn't pay then the big crime offenders had no chance. Today, New York is no longer the crime capital of the world and areas where people were afraid to go out at any time of the day are now teeming with people even after dark.

Karnam Malleswari, the Sydney Olympic medallist, has asked for a memorial to be built for the youngsters who died in the accident. That is a good thought and should help in easing the pain and sorrow that the family members must be feeling. The hopes, aspirations and ambitions they would have had for their children are gone and a memorial would alleviate to some extent their irreparable loss. But what they would want more than anything else is that no other families go through the trauma and sorrow that they are undergoing. That can only happen if the authorities take traffic violation seriously and have another look at how motor training schools are training their driving students.

A public awareness campaign by the big advertisers would also go a long way in making people more conscious of the need to observe road regulations whether one is a driver or a pedestrian. Top cricketers who are endorsing cars and car-care products could play a big role in moulding the future and new drivers by telling them through advertising campaigns the virtues of correct driving and observing the traffic rules. When such a campaign was once suggested to the chairman of a lubricant company he turned around and asked 'why would people believe a cricketer about traffic rules?' To this I could only reply because you expect the people to believe that the same cricketer knows which oil is for a car engine. It is not about knowledge but about credibility and apart from using celebrities for their campaign, if they also did an educational one with the same celebrity then it would definitely help. Trying to show the virtues of a car by making the celebrity take a u-turn and drive any which way without even giving any signal or indicator may make for a good commercial but it encourages young people to try and do that and while the celebrity has done all that through computer graphics and in a controlled environment, the impressionable youth may try to do it on a busy road and kill themselves and others in the process. Agencies which come up with slogan like 'make your own road' only encourage those vehicle owners to drive any which way they want.

Too many lives have been lost, too many budding careers nipped due to non-observance of the road rules. Let us all resolve to do something rather than pay lip service. That would be the best tribute to those whom the gods took away so prematurely.

27.09.2001

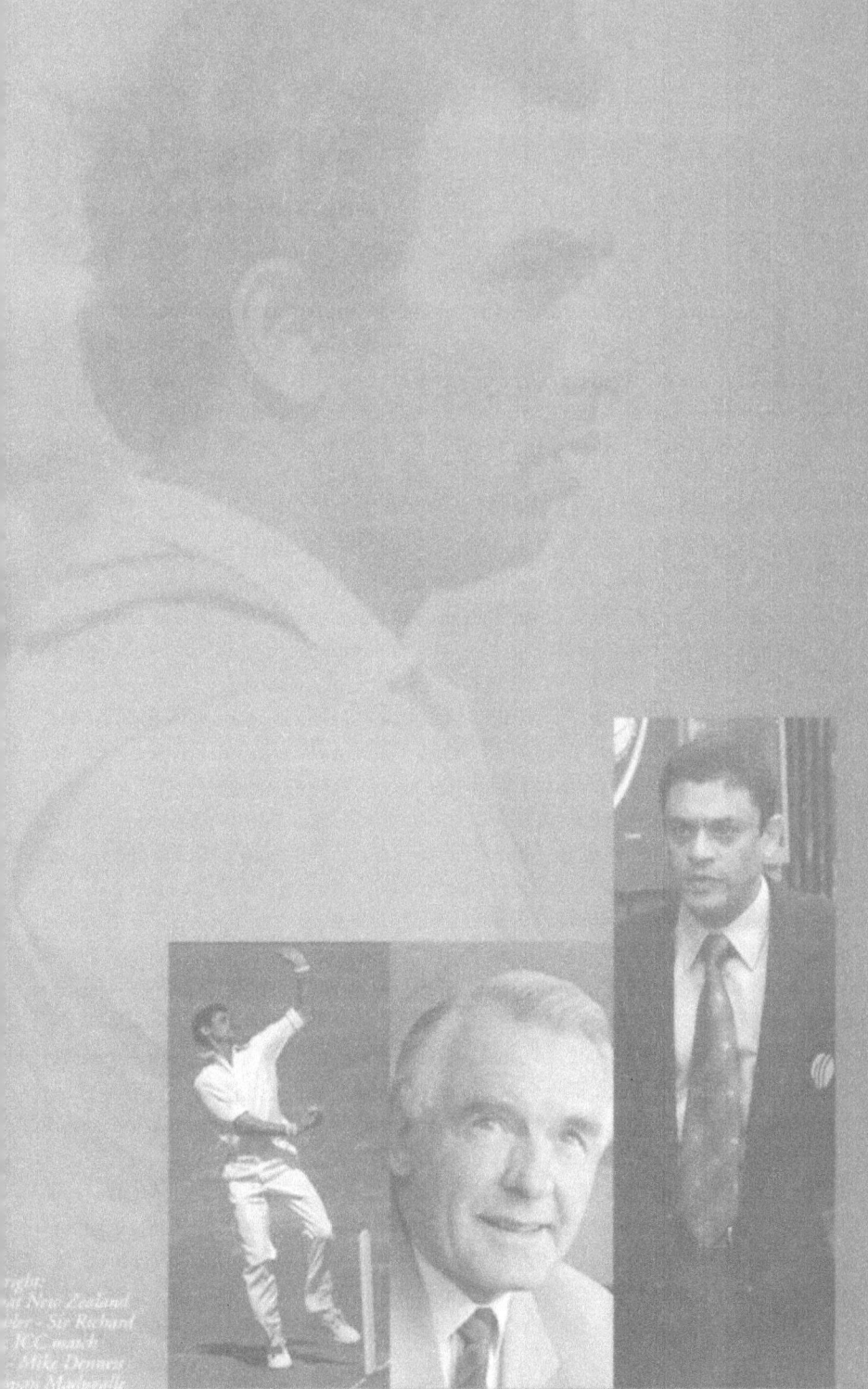

*right:
...t New Zealand
...der - Sir Richard
...ICC match
... Mike Denness
...son Mahingelle*

THE PROBLEM with Cricket Administration

I pen down these lines and in the days of laptops that's exactly what I am doing in spite of having my laptop with me. It has been virtually impossible to get a connection from the hotel I am in, so it's back to the good old longhand writing. This may well be an isolated happening for others may be getting connected. What definitely is not isolated is the hassle the Indian media has had to undergo for there are no dedicated lines for them at the grounds and so they have had to take the help of their South African colleagues or rush back to the hotels to send their copy and considering the time difference and the deadlines to meet it has been pretty stressful, to say the least. In spite of these troubles and the non-availability of fax machines for most of the tour for the regional language press to send their dispatches, the Indian media has hardly made a noise about it, at least publicly. Just imagine the same thing happening in India to the overseas media; the whole world and its aunt would have been told how it is impossible to get any decent facilities in India and our own media would have joined in the criticism. 'Tigers at home and lambs abroad' is not an exclusive tag for the Indian cricketers!!!

That's why it was so good to see the way the Indian media got behind the team after the sentences were announced by the match referee and it proves once again that it takes either a war or a calamity to get the Indians together. The scenes at the press conference where the match referee Mike Denness was subjected to a barrage of questions does bring into focus the ICC regulation that forbids the referee from speaking to the media about his decisions and why he took them. The media rightly asked that if the referee was not going to answer questions, why were they called? A press release would have been the better course of action rather than a press conference where a match referee cannot even explain his point of view. The ugly scenes that were seen around the cricketing world and even where cricket is not a major sport could then have been avoided.

At the time of writing, the ICC has indicated that the match referee will not be changed, neither will the decisions taken by him be kept in abeyance for a review and that puts the ball firmly back in the Indian Board's course. By the time this appears in print, we will have known whether cricket has won. Unfortunately, there are plenty of people in decision-making areas who have old

ICC match referee Ranjan Madugalle with the two captains, Australia's Ricky Ponting and India's Anil Kumble during the infamous India's tour of Australia.

scores to settle and axes to grind and that does not augur well for a decision in the game's interest, but the world is full of surprises and though there may well be a digging of heels, finally any decision will be made from the head and not the heart. What is needed is a statesman-like approach, but then how many sports administrators have this attribute?

What this whole episode does underscore is the urgency to have the elite panel of umpires and match referees in place much before the targeted date of 1 April 2002. The cricketing world simply cannot afford to lurch from one controversy to another, and an elite panel which has the confidence of the players will ensure to a great extent that episodes like this will be very very rare. As of now, every cricket board nominates two persons to be on the ICC referees' panel and it's from these that the ICC decides the postings to the various series played around the world. Not all, but there are some nominations which have to do with the local politics and power equations of that country's Board. So, honourable men that they are and without casting the least bit of aspersions on them and their capabilities they may not be the best nor would they be the ones to evoke respect from the players. It is, therefore, perhaps important for the ICC to go beyond these nominations and look at ex-players of repute who will have the players' respect and their admiration too. Somebody like a Clive Lloyd, a Majid Khan, a G.R. Vishwanath, an Allan Border, a Sir Richard Hadlee are some ex-players who have been giants during their time and whose integrity is beyond question. Having played some hard, closely fought matches during their time, they will understand much better how committed players can be and how sometimes in their fierce desire to do well for their country and team, they will show passion and emotion but which does not mean questioning the umpires' authority nor doubting his ability. An elite panel of umpires in any case will be able to nip in the bud any player who is getting carried away and out of hand by having a quiet word and not making too much of fuss about it.

Ranjan Madugalle has already been appointed the Chief Match Referee by the ICC and he is to go around the cricketing world to interact with the nominated persons by the various Boards to find others who will join him on the elite panel of five match referees. It is not going to be an easy decision to make and definitely harder than composing the elite umpires' panel. At least for the umpires there is a marking system by the captains and the match referees, which will be taken into account but there is nothing similar for the referees. That's why the suggestion to look beyond the nominations.

The quicker it is done the better, for there is a potentially controversial tour of India on at the moment, what with the happenings before the English team finally decided to tour. With the British media already showing that it has come with pre-conceived notions and closed minds and with their antipathy to the BCCI president as clear as daylight, the potential for a spark to ignite into a flame is enormous.

Hopefully, better sense will prevail and cricket will come out on top.

22.11.2001

REMEMBER, Who Started It

The ICC President Malcolm Gray has started a most commendable practice of meeting the various international teams, its officials and members before a Test or One-day series. A meeting like this not only lets the teams know of the work and the initiatives taken by the ICC but it also allows for interaction between the players and the officials. The one major snag that leads to avoidable problems has been the lack of communication between those who play the game and those who administer it and the ICC president's initiative does go a long way in bridging the communication gap. Most teams have taken this interaction to talk about the problems that are peculiar to that country and it does make for a better understanding of what makes some teams tick and some don't.

Having met the Australian, South Africa and New Zealand teams before the triangular series in Australia and then the teams playing in the ICC under-19 Cup, the president took the opportunity of being in New Zealand for an ICC meeting to catch up with the England team. And guess what the team or its officials did? They whinged about my column. Imagine that, here's a rare chance to meet with the ICC top brass and apprise them about the cricketing issues that they may have and they just confirm their unbeatable status as whingers.

England's Zimbabwean coach suggested that being on the ICC panel I should have an unbiased opinion and then added a personal remark about old wine. While I will not stoop to that level, please remember who started the unnecessary personal references if anything does happen in the future. Normally I don't react to the comments of others, as I believe that each is entitled to his or her opinion whether one agrees with those remarks or not and whether they are true or incorrect. But now having moaned to the ICC president it is about time to nail this canard that is being spread about a 'conflict of interests' between my media work and being on the ICC panel.

Nothing that I do in the media, both electronic and print, comes in the way of my work as the chairman of the ICC Cricket Committee, which in any case meets just once a year. That is a committee that looks at the laws and playing conditions of the game in the main. I am not the only member of the committee and there are more than ten others and a fair sprinkling of them including Allan Border are doing

Former ICC Chief Executive Malcolm Speed with the former ICC Presidents Malcolm Gray and Ehsan Mani.

media work. There's, therefore, no way it's a conflict of interests as was confirmed to me by the ICC chief executive Malcolm Speed. There was something he said that delighted me but I won't go into that here.

The previous evening too, at a convivial dinner the ICC president had remarked about my column which again heartened me and I would suggest to the England coach that he should perhaps check with the Australians. The New Zealanders, the West Indians, the Pakistanis, the Sri Lankans, the Bangladeshis, the South Africans and other Zimbabweans realise that it's something the whole world has been saying for years and not just me. Who knows before he was appointed coach he may well have had the same views. He, of course, very cleverly avoided talking about the instances that led me to make that comment but what is amusing is that when I wrote good things about their cricket, they obviously felt that there was no conflict of interest. When I wrote critical stuff then, *voila*, there was a conflict of interests.

The other amusing aspect of the whole thing was the way some in the media in England and the odd one in India tried to suggest that since I was not a destroyer of bowling, I should not be writing about the boring aspect of England team. As usual, when they have no argument to fall on they bring out the 36 not out in the first World Cup game forgetting that when I finished my career I had progressed to score the second fastest century in the world cup till then. Trying to make the case that the one has not done the same thing and so should not comment, is an argument that may well explode in their faces for then not having played the game at all apart from a very low level, the question is, should they be writing at all?

One more thing that is regularly brought up is the over-rate of the Indian team in the 1981-82 series conveniently forgetting that in the Oval Test in 1979 when India were chasing a target of 438, England bowled at a slovenly rate as soon as they realised they were not going to dismiss it. In fact, in the half hour after tea on the last day before the commencement of the 20 mandatory overs, they bowled only five overs. India's over-rate in 1981-82 was better than that but while Brearley was hailed as a master tactician for that, yours truly was made the villain. And let's not talk about the umpiring in that game either for those were 'human errors' by an English umpire unlike in the subcontinent when it would have been called 'cheating'.

So, now you see why I look at this entire thing as another example of British humour. I may not be a fan of their cricket but I am a big admirer of their humour.

14.02.2002

Indian captain
Ganguly, Indian
Javagal Srinath,
Siddhesh

THIS DILUTION is No Good

The ways of sports officialdom are hard to understand most times and one example of that is the stubbornness with which the Board of Control for Cricket in India (BCCI) refused to present the C.K.Nayudu Award to Subhash Gupte at his hometown in Trinidad. Gupte had been announced as the winner of the award which is given in recognition of services to Indian cricket, and the award presentation ceremony takes place at the Annual General Meeting of the Board which, as we all know, is really a battlefield for the different power blocs in the Board. So, straightway the importance of the Award gets diluted for the focus is more on the politicking and jockeying for power and the Award Ceremony is only a minor distraction for most since it involves a former cricketer. The administrators take pride in the fact that they have helped a 'poor' former cricketer get some money at this late stage of his life and so the honour of the Award also gets minimised for it's an Award for services and performance for Indian cricket and not dependent on the financial status of the awardee.

It was common knowledge that Subhash Gupte was not in the best of health. He was using a 'walker' to get about and was thus not very mobile. There was thus no way that he was going to be able to make the long journey to India. From Port of Spain to London is more than nine hours flying time and then from London to Mumbai is another nine hours. To ask a man struggling to walk to make that journey just to receive the Award was harsh, but then isn't he or wasn't he just a former cricketer, albeit one of Indian cricket's legends? It was suggested to the Board that the Award could be presented to Gupte when the Indian team was in Port of Spain and the manager or captain could give it to him. The Indian Board secretary was in Kingston for the last Test and he could have gone to Trinidad and presented the Award. Surely these were better options than to ask a man not in good health to make the long trip to India. Now that he is no more, hopefully the Board will send the Award and the money to his family quickly and not sit on it on some formality or the other. Sitting on the dues to players has been a very old practice of the Board and sometimes players get their tour fees almost a year after the tour is over and that too without any interest. It is a lot quicker now than in the past when players were even scared to ask for their fees for fear of being dropped from the next

Subhash Gupte showing his wizardry.

game. The usual excuse is that the manager has not submitted his reports and so the balance of the tour fees could not be paid to the players. The prize money too used to get delayed and all this while the Board was earning nice little interest on the players' money. Today of course the BCCI is very wealthy and does not have to resort to these methods but they were pretty much par for the course not too long ago.

Sourav Ganguly indicated in his press conference on arrival from the West Indies that he would try and persuade Javagal Srinath to reconsider his retirement. That will be an interesting conversation for during the just concluded Test series there seemed more than one occasion where the bowler did not see eye-to-eye with the captain and there was plenty of arms-flapping all round. The West Indies tour was a hard one and in those hot, humid conditions it was natural for a quick bowler to feel drained out and tired. The pitches were not much help either, particularly at Guyana and Antigua and later on at Jamaica, so the bowler with a longish run-up didn't find too much joy after all his efforts. It's not just Srinath but even Mervyn Dillon was looking jaded and worn out though, of course, being on the winning side makes a difference for it makes the effort worth it. Perhaps Srinath was just too tired and wanted out though he would have considered the fact that in England there would be no back-to-back Test matches and there would be plenty of opportunity to rest. Having played county cricket in England, Srinath also would be aware that English pitches are some of the slowest in the world and by July it can get hot in England and there won't be too much grass on the pitches either. So it would have been as much of a toll as in the West Indies and unless he got support from the other end, it would have been another innings of 400-plus to bowl through.

The strange thing is that Srinath has made himself available for the One-day matches where he has not been that effective. There, of course, he would be bowling only ten overs, but considering his batting has fallen desperately and he is not greased-lightning on the field, his usefulness in the limited-overs format is open to question. It really should have been the opposite where he was available for the Tests but not the One-dayers, for at the end of the day it is Test performances that leave an imprint, not the One-day deeds which are usually forgotten when the next One-dayer starts. Still, it is only he who knows his body and his mental strength and so we must respect his decision and thank him for the way he has bowled his heart out on some pretty abysmal pitches. He was a rarity in Indian cricket, a genuine speedster who by dint of hard work went on to capture over 200 wickets and but for a shoulder injury that sidelined him for some time and no doubt reduced his pace by at least ten kilometers an hour, he would have gone on to capture over 300 wickets in Test cricket.

Well played Javagal Srinath, take a bow, the cricketing community applauds and appreciates your contribution to Indian cricket.

06.06.2002

English
a few
Player
Black Bands
solidarity

Why is it DIFFERENT ABROAD?

When a cricket team from overseas comes to India, is there an official from the Board of Control for Cricket in India (BCCI) to receive them? Yes.Does the Board official along with officials from the immigration and customs meet the team well before the team reaches the immigration counter? Yes.

Do the immigration officials collect the passports of all the players and officials and most times the media personnel accompanying the team? Yes.

Is the team then taken to the VIP lounge, given welcome drinks while their passports are stamped? Yes.

Do the porters collect the baggage from the arrival belt and load it into team coach? Yes.

Now instead of 'overseas cricket team' put the words 'Indian cricket team' and instead of 'visiting India' put the words 'when visiting overseas' and the answer to the same question will be 'no' every single time. Apart from in the West Indies, the Indian team has to stand in a queue like everybody else, their bags have to be collected by themselves, they have to, in some countries, even put money for a trolley and load the bags in the team bus themselves. That there was nobody from the New Zealand cricket to assist the team and liaise with the immigration and the customs is something the BCCI must take up most strongly. Sure, there is not the same following for the sport as in India and nobody is suggesting that the law of the land be broken, but surely the fines could have been waived if New Zealand cricket officials had been there.

Tell me, if an overseas player coming to India had a minor infringement like the Indians had on arrival in New Zealand, would not that have been taken care of by the Board Officials and the immigration and customs? They would have at best reprimanded the offender, not fined him, for sporting teams are our guests and we treat our guests well. It is the 'fine' aspect that is bothersome. It is not the amount for the Indians will probably spend more than ten times the amount in New Zealand, but the embarrassment that it has caused. It was the captain Sourav Ganguly no less who was fined and that is hard to accept. No visiting captain to India will ever get treatment like this whatever be the infringement.

In view of what has happened, perhaps it's time to reassess the way we treat our visitors. If our players are getting no special treatment, the same must be the case with visitors. It's just not the hospitality, but little things like accessories for sport where the treatment varies. If an Indian player wants shoelaces for his cricket boots he will have to pay for them overseas, if he wants a rubber grip for his bat he will have to pay for it or a tape for repairing the bat he pays for it. When overseas teams come here, instead of one shoelace, the team will be given a dozen free of cost, so also for the rubber grips and bat tapes or any other cricketing accessory. Is that reciprocated? No, sir, and this is where we have to reassess our treatment.

Take, for example, our players standing for two minutes in silence in England when two schoolgirls were kidnapped and killed. It was a big story in England then but there are tragic stories in India too. Would the English team have stood for two minutes if there was a similar situation in India? But then the question is whether the Indian team itself would have stood for an Indian tragedy? They did not wear black armbands when the vice-president passed away but were happy to stand for two minutes for two school girls whom they did not even know. Talking of black armbands, the Pakistanis also wore them along with the Australians to mourn the deaths of Australian tourists in the explosion in Bali. The question is, would the Australians wear black armbands if people from the subcontinent are killed somewhere? One might argue that it's a human thing but the counter question is, is it only human when people from certain countries are affected? When are we, in the subcontinent, going to get over this complex of trying to please these people and earning brownie (excuse the pun) points from them?

Coming to cricket, it was refreshing to read the statement of Dilip Vengsarkar, the chairman of the Mumbai Cricket Association selection committee, Chandu Pandit, the coach and Paras Mahambrey, the captain about the new-ball prospect, Aviskar Salvi. While Vengsarkar said that he needs to be tested against quality batsmen, both Pandit and Mahambrey said that though he is a great prospect, he is a bit raw and needs to be moulded. How good it was to see this maturity when everybody else is just trying to push their favourites even before they are ready.

On the day the selection of the Indian team was made, there was an agency report cleverly planted from Hyderabad about young Ambati Rayudu being the youngest double centurion in the Ranji Trophy and so should be picked up for the national squad. Not a word about him getting a pair of zeroes in the game against Mumbai, a better bowling team than Andhra Pradesh. It is this unholy rush that will cause more problems than waiting for a couple of season's experience in domestic cricket that will prepare them for the sterner Tests of international cricket. But if that could be put down to over-enthusiasm, what about two mothers who came down to Mumbai to meet the selectors for their sons' inclusion in the team to New Zealand, probably mistaking it for a school admission? They were lucky that this selection committee consists of gentlemen who would not take advantage. However, it just goes to show the stakes involved if mothers have to do this. By the way, both players were not selected.

05.12.2002

Enter **GREG CHAPPELL**

I t's been quite interesting to hear and read the stories regarding Greg Chappell's possible stint with the Indian team at its training camp in Bangalore before the new season gets underway. What is hard to understand is the controversy that is being sought to be created about John Wright's position as the Indian coach if Chappell does come to India. There is absolutely nothing wrong if a coach feels that his team will be better served if another specialist comes in to help the boys out with his experience and expertise. After all, the specialist is only an invitee and not a permanent coach, so where's the conflict with the national coach's position? If a former Indian player were to be asked to come and give his expertise to the batsmen, would it conflict with Wright's position? If not, then why will Chappell's visit, if in fact there's going to be a visit, clash with Wright's position and authority?

Even when Wright has been the coach, there have been others who have helped the boys whenever the boys have gone to them, notably Geoffrey Boycott and Mohinder Amarnath, to name a couple. Why, even I have had the pleasure of interacting with some of the players on specific areas of their batting when they have approached me.

What one must try and find out are the coach and Ganguly's reasons for wanting Greg Chappell. Is it because India is to visit Australia shortly? If that's the reason, then it's the wrong reason for quite simply, with all his greatness as a batsman, Chappell's thinking will be Australian and what the Indians need is Indian thinking. By that, I mean an Indian who has played pace well and knows how to approach the innings and succeed against them. To give you a simple example, an Australian batsman may think only ten times about tackling the short ball, while an Indian will think maybe twenty-five times. It's how to get rid of thinking and making the short ball work for you, that's the key and it can only be explained by an Indian who has gone through it and knows how to treat the demons in the mind about the short delivery. The Australians play pace day in and day out, and so don't think too much about it. The Indians, on the other hand, hardly get to play quality pace at home in domestic cricket and so find it harder to cope with it when they go on to international cricket.

But there have been some fine players who have gone on to bat exceedingly

Saurav Ganguly and Greg Chappell.

well against the quick stuff and got runs against it. Not too long ago, G.R.Vishwanath, Mohinder Amarnath, Dilip Vengsarkar and Ravi Shastri have all got loads of runs against the speedsters and they have done it after playing mainly slow bowlers in domestic cricket, so they know a thing or two about making that mental adjustment when they went to play Test cricket. These are the guys who should be talking to Indian team and even players like Kiran More and Shivlal Yadav, who battled it out against fearsome pace and did better than expected. They didn't say that they were not specialist batsmen and so didn't have to try. How they made the adjustment is what only they can tell and that's what some of the current guys need … that inspiration that they also can tackle pace although yes, it will be painful at times doing so.

If John Wright has indeed asked Greg to help out, he is being honest with Indian cricket, for he thinks that Greg will have some more to contribute than he can, but in no way does this dilute his authority and position as coach. Maybe he feels that there are certain aspects of batsmanship that are better explained by others. He is the coach not just for batting but for the all-round approach and attitude of the Indians to their different opponents. He has no ego hassles about his team members asking some other former players for help and that's his strength in that he sees what's good for Indian cricket rather than what's good for John Wright.

Greg Chappell's presentation at a recent seminar was very impressive according to those who attended it, but remember he was talking mainly to coaches who have the juniors as their wards. There is still some scope to make changes to the techniques of juniors, but virtually impossible to do so once a player is about eighteen years old, for by then he is set in the way he moves, whether batting or bowling. Where players like Greg Chappell and Geoffrey Boycott will be invaluable is in their interaction with the junior cricketers whose technique is still at a malleable stage. That, along with the temperament, is what will eventually make the difference between good First-class players and good international players. Now that Geoffrey Boycott is well, it would be a great idea to have him come down to the NCA. Sure, he can talk to the current squad as well, but there's not much that one can do to change their technique, for it's formed and hardly possible to change. Yes, one can make minor corrections, but the major ones are in the mind. And here, with all due respect, it's only those who have gone into international cricket with the same kind of mind and conquered it who can help, and these are former Indian players.

To tell from personal experience, I had the good fortune of representing my country for more than a few years and tour all cricketing countries, during which there was lot of interaction with the players and officials of those countries as well as former greats there. But the best advice I got was from former Indian players. Nobody, not even the greatest of middle-order batsmen 'sir DGB' was able to give me the tips that the former Indian greats did. There were four tips that were invaluable. The first was from my uncle Madhav Mantri who told me after a double century in an inter-collegiate game when I threw my wicket away that I should never do a favour to the bowler and to never throw my wicket away irrespective of the runs I have scored. The second was from Nari Contractor who told me to keep a diary especially of the days when I batted well and write in it everything from the sleep I had, to how I felt on waking up and going to ground, the walk to the pitch, the stance, the grip, the movement of the feet, just about everything. He said it would help when I was in a bad patch, for not only it would get my self-belief back but also tell me what I had done to bat well that day.

The third was from the late Vinoo Mankad who told me at a reception to stop pointing my elbow towards the bowler in my stance as it hampered my on-side play. This was after I had a few Test centuries under my belt. Vinoobhai was our coach at college and so had seen me prior to my playing Tests. The fourth was from Polly Umrigar who told me that if I wanted to play long innings in our hot and humid conditions, then I must not waste my energy running fast for easy singles, unless of course there was a chance of another run. I kept all this advice in mind and though it wasn't always possible to follow it, there's not the slightest doubt that it did help me getting a few more runs in international cricket. I rest my case.

17.07.2003

INSPIRATION... More the Merrier!

By the time you read this, the conditioning camp for the probables to the Indian team will have begun. Considering the fact that most of the seniors in the Indian team have had more than four months away from the game, this is a good move by the Board to get the boys to now start thinking about the game after a well-deserved break. It will also give the players a chance to get to know the new physical trainer and vice versa, though of course Adrian Le Roux will have already filled him in on the varying stages of physical fitness and stamina and pain-threshold levels of the players. Every individual has his own limits physically and it is getting the best of these limits and slowly trying to expand and extend them, which is what the new trainer will no doubt try to strive for. There is no use trying to force a training programme down every player's throat, but to find out what's best for them to perform on the field at an optimum level.

Even as the physical conditioning gets underway, it would also be a great idea to have some mental conditioning, for it is this aspect that is crucial in a tight situation on the field. The India 'A' team which recently had a successful tour of England, had gone and met the Infosys Chief Mr N.R. Narayana Murthy during their camp in Bangalore prior to their departure. By all accounts, it was an inspirational meeting and if Narayana Murthy is free, then the probables can visit him again and come away that much more wiser.

If John Wright and Saurav Ganguly can also call other winners to meet up with the team and address them, then the camp will be more meaningful. Having the likes of Prakash Padukone who is a local man and other champions like Pullela Gopichand, Michael Ferreira, Geet Sethi, Milkha Singh drop in at the camp and speak to the probables will be a fantastic morale-booster. They can speak from experience about how they came back from hopeless situations to win their games, or how they coped with pressure situations and came out on top. Here it is not just a question of skill, but how that skill allied to temperament helped them overcome their opponent. While Ferreira and Sethi can tell them about the way to stay positive even when things are looking bleak, Prakash, Gopichand and Milkha Singh can tell them how when the lungs and legs are saying enough and the body is feeling dead, they kept the mind's eye focused on the goal of winning and so propelled

Saurav Ganguly and John Wright.

the extra superhuman effort that took them to the winners' podium. These are things that cannot be taught through books but can only be imbibed being inspired by those who have actually experienced it.

If Wright can get mountaineers or long-distance runners also to the camp to speak of their experiences, then it could well be the most productive camp the BCCI has ever had. Expense is not a problem and the BCCI can well afford to not only fly in these champions but also give them an honorarium for their contribution. If Leander Paes and Mahesh Bhupathi are around, they could also be invited, but presumably they will be away preparing for the US Open which starts in a few days' time.

After the conditioning camp is over, there is a break for a few days and then the cricket camp starts. Here too, it might be a good idea to invite the likes of Kapil Dev, Mohinder Amarnath, Viswanath, Vengsarkar and Shastri to visit the camp and be on hand for any technical help that the players might need. Erapalli Prasanna, Chandrasekhar and B.S. Bedi who have had successful trips Down Under could also give invaluable tips on how to bowl on pitches that aren't exactly spinner-friendly. This season is an important one since it affords India an opportunity to beard the lion in its own den and also every possible help should be sought to ensure that the campaign is successful. Sure, too many cooks can spoil the broth, but a judicious blend can make it tastier as well.

Hopefully, the Indians will also be inspired by the way the young South African captain has silenced the doubters with his awesome batting. Who knows, by the time this is in print, he may well have scored a third consecutive double century and that will put him in a class by himself. When he was appointed captain, there were many who questioned the appointment, but he has with great determination and personal example shown his team how to pile on not just the runs, but pressure as well. The others who have scored back-to-back double tons have all been middle-order batsmen. Smith not only took the brave decision to bat first in the first Test on a pitch which has helped seamers in the early part of the first day, but also took the bold one of putting England in, in the second Test. The latter decision was criticised by the experts who felt that there was no juice in the pitch, nor any help from the conditions to warrant a decision like that. Smith proved them wrong as his bowlers ran through the English batting and dismissed them before the close of play on the first day itself, and then ground them with his second consecutive double century that led to their victory and gave South Africa a lead in the series. With three more Tests to go, Smith has the opportunity to be the first to score 1000 runs in a five-Test series. The closest has been Sir Don Bradman with 974 runs, and Smith with 621 runs already has a very good chance to eclipse that and be the first to score 1000.

Even that will not convince that perennial doubter Barry Richards who expressed the view that Smith should be seen against Australia before being deemed great. Why only Australia, why not on the spinning pitches of the subcontinent? Richards even questioned Tendulkar's greatness in spite of the fact that the little champion has scored hundreds against the best and in their countries too. While the little champion, as is his wont, has let his bat do the talking, the fiery South African captain is not known to mince his words as can be seen by his comments about Lance Klusener. So, it wouldn't be a surprise if Smith turns around and asks Richards how he can be called great when he never played the West Indian pace attack at its fiercest, nor did he bat against the spin quarter of India in the subcontinent, and scored his runs against an Australian attack which was jaded and tired after an energy-sapping tour of India. That South Africa was isolated from sport is no excuse, nor cricket history is littered with examples of debut series wonders, who went out of cricket not too long after.

14.08.2003

Yet Another **TRAGIC TALE**

The outpouring of good wishes for the speedy recovery of Jugraj Singh, Indian hockey's young lion, shows that the game is back in the hearts of Indian sports lovers. Though cricket may be the more popular sport, there is no doubt that the national game is hockey and the performance of the hockey teams—both senior and junior as well as the women's teams in recent times—has brought great cheer to the sporting community. Jugraj's unfortunate accident has dampened that a fair bit as it means that one of Indian hockey's brightest stars is not going to be fit enough to don the national colours for a long time and may even miss next year's Olympics in Athens.

This might be as good a time as any to reflect why our highways are death traps and accidents have snuffed out some brilliant careers from all walks of life and not just sports. It is not a question of whether Jugraj was at fault or not, but the fact is road accident fatalities around the country are quite high in the list of cases of deaths, apart from illnesses. How regularly do we read about marriage parties losing entire families in road accidents? How often we read about school buses taking children for picnics, getting into accidents? The point is, all these are avoidable if the traffic rules were obeyed, but the Indian driver is always in a hurry and will cut corners to reach his destination and in the process, cause accidents and loss to either his family or that of others. The Highway Code is observed more in the breach than anything else, simply because there is no fear of the law and any subsequent punishment. It is not just on the highways that there is danger to life, but also on the city roads, though because of heavy traffic and thus slowing down the speed, the accidents are more a threat to limbs than life.

The sad part is that it is the professional driver who is the culprit in the majority of the traffic misdemeanours. Yes there are others too, especially teenagers who have just got their licenses and get carried away, but in the main it is the guy who earns his living plying vehicles who is in the forefront of breaking traffic rules. Just take a look at the taxi drivers and truck drivers on the highways and you will know what I mean. And in Mumbai the BEST bus drivers are a law unto themselves. When was the last time you saw a BEST driver being hauled up by a traffic cop for breaking the rules? And what of our generation next which apes everything

Mansur Ali Khan 'Tiger' Pataudi.

that the West has, like jeans, beer and pub culture but is averse to following the way most drivers in the West generally follow the traffic rules. Why, one has to be a mind reader on Indian roads for, in spite of the latest gadgetry in the cars, few drivers care to give the cars behind a signal that they are going to turn right or left and cutting into lanes without signals is almost like the birthright of most drivers. Another irritating habit is driving with full beam lights on at night, instead of using the dipper. It's almost as if the drivers are in collusion with opticians to give them more business for damaged eyes. Even Mumbai which is one of those cities where drivers use dipper, is now using full head lights and on well-lit roads too probably due to more outsiders in the city than ever before. Driving is no longer a pleasure, be it on city roads with the awful conditions they are in and on the highways where there is the fear that another idiot might cause you serious injury.

Have a look at some of the names who have been seriously injured or killed in road accidents and you will see why it is important that something be done very quickly to ensure another family is not left in misery. From the cricketing world, the death of 'Collie Smith', one of West Indian cricketers' most promising all-rounders, the accident to Colin Milburn and to our very own 'Tiger' Pataudi where he lost one eye. Just imagine what a player Tiger Pataudi would have been with two eyes, if he could bat so brilliantly with just one. On the political front too, the loss of Rajesh Pilot, one of the most hard-working and promising politicians, the death of Bindumadhav Thackeray and in hockey itself the death of the great Surjit Singh, are enough reasons for the Road Safety Department to take matters seriously to ensure that accidents are kept to a minimum by a strict application of the traffic laws. Perhaps they should start by having a media campaign with some of the luminaries in India exhorting the people to observe the traffic laws. A print media and electronic media campaign will definitely make a difference, though of course it will not be easy to change the approach and attitude overnight. One tends to ignore the danger of road accidents till it happens to someone close in your family or friends' circle, but if the hazards are brought out then it will make for much safer and enjoyable driving in the country.

The automobile industry is one of the biggest spenders on advertising and if they can be persuaded to combine the virtues of their vehicle—be it a two or a four wheeler—with tips on good safe driving, they will be doing a great social service along with promoting their vehicles. So also the oil companies and tyre manufacturers.

Slogans like 'Own the road or make your own road' only encourage bad driving and may lead to accidents, so the advertising companies also could do a lot of good if they looked more carefully into promoting a safer driving environment than just looking for trashy catchy lines.

You may be tempted to say that the majority of the Indians do not own cars. Yes, that is true, but there is public transport and that too could do with better driving habits.

Jugraj's family is lucky that he is still there but some other family may not be so fortunate. So, please think about it and observe traffic rules, drive safely and go home to your family.

11.09.2003

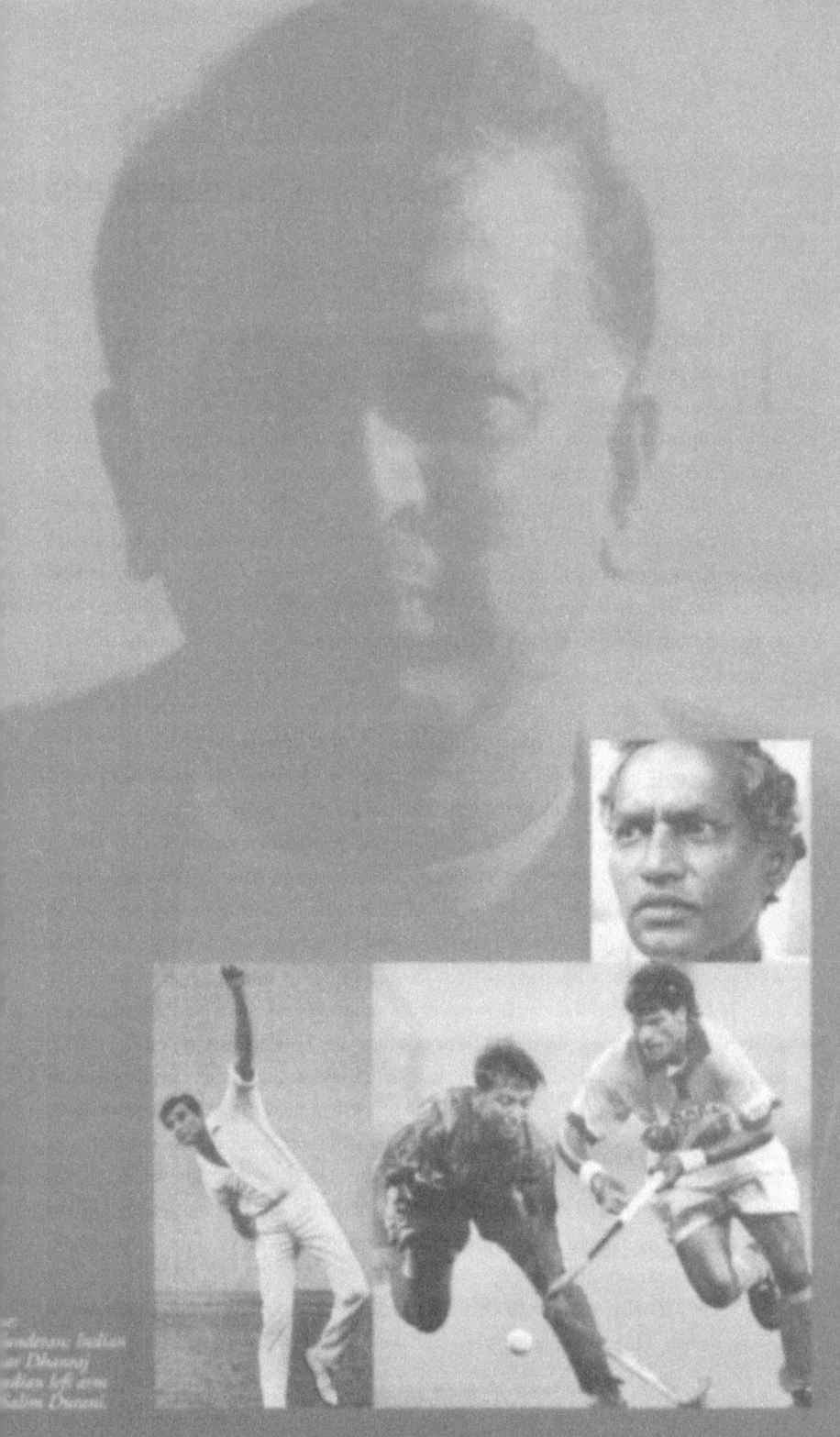

*Wonderous Indian
...ar Dhanraj
...dian left arm
...alim Durani*

BUDHI and The Golden Age

I t was so good to read about Budhi Kunderan being back in Mumbai, though it was sad to read that this would be his last visit to India. Having settled in Scotland and being retired now, one can understand that it is not easy to travel long distances in spite of the enormous progress in the aviation industry in terms of flight, fares, comfort, time taken, etc. Budhi belonged to that generation of Indian Cricket which in my humble view is the Golden Age of Indian cricket. I suppose, to a teenager growing up with stars in his eyes, the heroes of the day will always remain heroes forever and Budhi certainly was one of them. What a golden period it was in Indian cricket in the 1960s! The dashing Nawab of Pataudi had taken over as the captain of the team at the tender age of twenty-one after the unfortunate injury to his captain. Under him, the team underwent a change of image from being dull pushovers to those who could look anybody in the eye and play some fabulous cricket. Pataudi himself with the peak of his cap pulled rakishly over his damaged right eye had with him dashers like M.L. Jaisimha, Farokh Engineer, Salim Durani, Budhi Kunderan, Chandu Borde and Hanumant Singh. It was a team of handsome men and even today, to talk to the then teenaged girls of that time and see their faces soften at the memory of these good lookers in creams, is a sight to behold. There was the spin combination coming to the fore too, in Prasanna, Bedi, Venkatraghavan and Chandrasekhar who also fascinated all those who watched them with their incredible skill and the cunning with which they got the batsmen out. To watch them in the nets was a delight and an education in itself, for these were no ordinary nets where the bowlers just rolled their arms over and the batsmen had a slog. The new-ball bowlers like Ramakant Desai, Rusi Surti and Abid Ali may not have been express, but bowling a little less than 22 yards, they were not afraid to let go more than the odd bouncer even if it was to the captain Pataudi and seniors like Chandu Borde. Then the laughter at the end of a good session left all those watching like yours truly also leave with a big grin on their faces. Why even as I write this, there is a silly smile on my face just thinking back at those wonderful days.

The BCCI tried its best to control the guys after playing hours but it was a losing battle. There were escapades that were recounted with great hilarity and apart from the odd one, nothing ever became public. What was clear was that those guys played some hard cricket and then partied hard later. The results on the field were not exactly brilliant, but really who gave a damn for these were some real special guys who the public longed to be near to.

I have been out of town for most of the time since I returned from Australia and even this is being written from out of town, so am not sure if I will be able to meet Budhi before he goes away, but if he does read this, all I will add is, 'Thank you for the excitement you and your generation brought to me when I was growing up and wanting to be a cricketer.' I hope Budhi will change his mind about this being his last visit to India, for he may not know it but there are several more like me who are nostalgic about that Golden Age in Indian cricket and want the Kunderans, Engineers, Abid Alis to keep coming back.

In another sport, there is someone who brings to hockey the same kind of flavour and flair that Pataudi and his team of the 1960s did and is perhaps paying the price for it and that person is none other than the irrepressible Dhanraj Pillay. His game is the same dashing one of Pataudi and company and brings in spectators to watch this mercurial player, but just like those players did not really care two hoots about the administration then, so does Dhanraj not really worry too much about officialdom. He has got into so many scraps with authority that perhaps there is never a big hockey event complete unless there is some news on Dhanraj. Whether he was not wanted by some section of the team or whether he felt he himself was not yet fully fit is not clear, but the fact is that the Indian hockey team has left for the Olympic qualifier event without him. Dhanraj is utterly dedicated to Indian hockey and if he felt he was not fully fit for such an important tournament then he needs to be complimented for his honesty in putting Indian hockey first and not just going on a free trip overseas. Indian cricket could do with such honesty for claims are made by players on their behalf by their people that they are fit when they are not. There are innumerable instances of these to fill more than one column, so suffice it to say that the BCCI must follow the Australian method with those who have been unfit with injury.

In Australia, even proven match-winners like Shane Warne and Glenn McGrath have to play in a first-class or a One-dayer interstate game to show that they are fully fit. It's not just playing the game but the days after to see how their bodies, especially the injured parts, have responded to the rigours of a proper game that is taken into account before they are considered for the national team. In Warne's case, there was no injury but he was coming into big-time cricket after a twelve-month ban and so the selectors wanted to see how he would cope with such a long lay-off. There was great media-hype about his return which was for a second XI and it was only after he played a first-class game, bowled plenty of overs, took some wickets that he was picked to be part of the Australian team that will play Tests in Sri Lanka after the limited-overs series is over. Glenn McGrath claimed he was fit to play Tests but inspite of his terrific record, the selectors did not consider him as he had not played any matches after his injury where they could see how he bowled and how his injury reacted to bowling in match conditions. He may well be bowling without a problem in the nets, but as far as the selectors are concerned, they wanted him to prove his fitness in a match and not just in the nets, never mind if he has got over 400 wickets in Test cricket.

The BCCI will hopefully tell its selectors to do what the Australian selectors do and to see the injured player in a proper game and not go by what the player himself says or a certificate that he gets from a doctor. In a country where there is fake stamp paper, what price a fitness certificate?

One of the reasons that the Australians are World Champions is because the best of their players cannot take their places for granted in the team. They have to perform consistently and meet the required fitness standards and only then can they get the pleasure of wearing the baggy green cap.

The BCCI, which is moving in a more professional direction, will do well to impose the same standards for their players so that they continue to do well for India rather than stick to their places of some performance in the past.

26.02.2004

Kumble Should **COUNT HIMSELF LUCKY**

The much maligned BCCI needs to be congratulated on giving permission to Anil Kumble to visit his wife and to be present when she gave birth to their son. Kumble had just bowled India to a historic win over Pakistan and added to that was the joy of being a father a couple of days later. Whether the BCCI would have allowed Kumble to visit his wife if India had not done well in the Test is a matter of conjecture, but the very fact that permission was given shows that the BCCI recognises that the family is an important factor in a cricketer's life. The players play so much and travel so much that the family life is virtually non-existent for some, and even when they are in India, there are so many functions to attend that it's hard for players to spend quality time with their loved ones. The BCCI has also allowed the players' wives to join them on long tours, but after the first few weeks when players are going through the drill of acclimatising practice routines and other official functions that are a part of a touring team's schedule. Nowadays, even that has been cut down and so the functions the team has to attend are fewer than say ten years ago.

Kumble being allowed to return home to be in time for his wife's delivery takes me many years back when in a similar situation, I wasn't allowed to return to India to see my new born son even though I was injured and unable to play for a few weeks. Of course, New Zealand wasn't as geographically close to India as Pakistan is, but still BCCI flatly refused to give me permission to return home even at my own expense. I had sustained a broken cheekbone while fielding at forward short-leg and so was ruled out of playing for a few weeks. Fortunately for me, we were to go to the West Indies directly from Kiwiland, and the Tests there were to start after a few weeks while the team played a few first-class games against the islands. So, there was enough time to return home, see my son and then go rejoin the team. Amazingly, while the BCCI denied me permission to return home, they allowed me to stay on in USA along with the assistant manager Balu Alaganan and then rejoin the team a few days before the first Test at Barbados. It was disappointing to say the least, as it was another two months before I saw and held my son in my hands for the first time, and it was quite absurd to let me be in America but not go to India.

Anil Kumble with his better half Chetana.

Different cricket boards have different rules, but the most forward-thinking board is the South African board, which not only allows the players' wives or partners as they are referred to in the Western world to join them at some pre-agreed stage of the tour but also pays for their travel and boarding and lodging. That may be a bit too much to hope for in India, but at least the thinking is not as rigid as it was even ten years back.

The BCCI was ruled with an iron hand in those days and it was on that tour to the West Indies that the first ever cricket association was born. It was also the most successful of associations, for the BCCI quickly realised the unity of the players and began to make more concessions and hear out the players more than ever before. Many a legitimate concern of the players was accepted and though as in the present case, there was no official recognition of the players' body, there was unofficial contact with the BCCI officials, who, when approached with player's concerns, were quick to take responsive measures. Today, thanks to the widespread interest in the game and thanks to media interest, the BCCI is no longer the ogre that it was then, and nobody in the BCCI looks upon it as his personal fiefdom to do as he pleases and play with the careers of players.

While not entirely professional and still not totally accountable, the BCCI is today far more forward-thinking than in its early years. Though it may still be run by administrators who have not all played at the highest level, there is a greater awareness of players' needs and how to address the various problems that the players might have. If today, India has gone on to win a Test in Pakistan for the first time and also won the limited-overs series, then recognition must be given to the vision displayed by the BCCI in insisting that the limited-overs be played first and Tests later. The Pakistan Cricket Board was keen to have the Tests first and then the ODIs, saying that there would be not many spectators if the Tests were played later and they are being proved right, but the BCCI stuck to its guns and saw that India played the ODIs first. This was simply because the Indians were coming after a limited-over series in Australia and would be in that frame of mind which would not help their cricket; as it turns out, the Indians have not only won the limited-overs series but also gone on to win the first Test where many a Pakistani dismissal was because their inexperienced players were still in the One-day mode and did not go on to build their innings as is required in a Test match. At the time of writing this, Pakistan is looking good to level the series, but at least India has broken the jinx of never having won a Test in Pakistan. The BCCI deserves credit for sticking to its gun and making that win possible.

There is ample scope for improvement in the BCCI but at least there is an acceptance that the players are more important than the administrators. It's the beginning but there is still someway to go before the BCCI becomes truly professional and truly transparent but at least a start has been made and for that we all must be thankful to the administrators who made it so.

08.04.2004

LARA'S 400 and All That

In the Western world quite often the question is asked, 'Where were you when JFK was assassinated?' or 'where were you when Princess Diana died in a car crash?' In India it is more likely to be 'where were you when Mrs. Indira Gandhi was killed or where were you when Rajiv Gandhi was blown up by assassins?' On the cricketing front, the question would perhaps be 'where were you when India won the World Cup in 1983?' or more recently 'where were you when India beat Pakistan to win the series?' If you are not an Indian fan, then you might query where were you when Brian Lara became the first cricketer to score 500 runs in an innings in first-class cricket? Or, where were you when Brian Lara became the first batsman to score a quadruple century in Test cricket?

These are special moments in cricket history and even if one was not there to witness it personally, to be able to recall where one was adds to the significance of the moment and the occasion. So, where were you when Lara scored his 400th run?

I was at a friend's house watching it on TV and it was an awe-inspiring moment. What was remarkable was the way he kept his focus even after regaining the batting record of 380 that Mathew Hayden had scored just six months earlier. How often have batsmen been out immediately after reaching a personal milestone like 50 or a century or 150? That's because the concentration and focus shifts just a little bit in acknowledging the applause of the crowd, savouring the achievement and a bit of relaxation creeps into the game in the next few minutes, till the concentration comes back to its intense level before the milestone was reached. Once that happens, then the batsmen goes on to the next milestone, but it is in those few minutes before the intensity of focus returns, when every batsman is vulnerable and tends to get out. So, if Lara had lost his concentration after getting to 381, especially after play was interrupted as the prime minister of Antigua walked onto the field to offer his congratulations, it would have been perfectly understandable, but Lara knew, ten years ago that he had missed out on the chance of becoming the first batsman to score 400 in a Test innings and this time he was not going to miss it.

It was quite amazing how, as one watched, one was urging him not to do anything silly as he approached first the Hayden score of 380 and then as he neared 400. Having said that, one has to admit that six months ago, when Hayden was

Brian Lara getting a guard of honour by his teammates after he set a new world batting record in Test cricket with 400 runs not out against England.

getting close to Lara's 375, it was exactly the same sense of anxiety. World records like that don't happen too often and that's why the spectator, irrespective of the nationality, also is mentally batting for the batsman who is getting to the record.

It was the same as Sehwag approached 300. Having got so close, one did not want him to miss out on being the first Indian to score a triple ton in Test cricket and the dasher obliged by hitting a huge six and getting there in style. Even then, the worry was that at Melbourne on 195, he had got out caught in the deep going for a six to get to a 200 and here he was on 295, looking to get to 300. It was hard not to keep smiling after that achievement, not just because it is a unique one in Indian cricket, but because the guy who got it is such a likeable guy and one felt extremely happy for him.

Lara's 400 helped to raise the mood in the West Indies after their team had lost the earlier three Tests quite ignominiously, being dismissed for 47 and 91 in two of the Tests. His innings gave the West Indians plenty to cheer about, apart from ensuring that there was no whitewash in the series. There were invariably some who felt that Lara's effort was not a team effort but a selfish one, but quite frankly, did the West Indians have the bowling power to dismiss England twice on such a good batting pitch? That England scored over 400 runs in the second innings with four of their wickets in hand shows how good the pitch was for batting on the last day. Don't forget also that there was time lost on the first couple of days because of rain, and so to blame Lara for batting on to score 400 is childish. Instead of complimenting him for his effort in that energy-sapping heat, these people are only throwing mud at him simply because of their personal likes and dislikes. It is no secret that because Lara gives back as good as he gets, he is not the most popular player in certain countries and it is from these countries that the criticism has come through. Sure, no personal achievement should take precedence over team interests, but pray tell me, how much time did Lara take to go from 381 to 400? Maybe twenty minutes and are we to believe that but for these twenty minutes, West Indies would have won? No way.

Brian Lara's consistency and appetite for big hundreds in recent years has been phenomenal and it will once again ignite the race to be recognised as the best batsman in the world. There are several contenders for the title, though of course it can hardly be final, since the opposition and playing conditions will continue to vary, but it will be great for the debates for each candidate's supporter to argue endlessly into the night. Sadly, the same doesn't happen with the bowlers of the world. No wonder it is called a batsman's game!

23.04.2004

Back in The **US OF A**

Being in the USA, one does not get much cricket but there is its cousin – Golf, which is pretty big and has a wide following. Golf is catching up in India as well and the encouraging performances of Jyoti Randhawa and Arjun Atwal, Jeev Milkha Singh and company is exciting for the followers of sport in our country. Sure, we need more golf courses for the game to grow, but in a developing country like ours, open spaces are usually used for housing and thus golf, which needs lots of room, is shifted to places outside the city, which doesn't make it easy for the common man to take it up. The cost of golfing equipment is also high and so it's not a game that parents will encourage their kids to take up.

Having just seen Vijay Singh falter in a tournament where he and Ernie Els had the chance to topple Tiger Woods from his number one spot that Tiger has held since August 1999, makes one wonder whether cricket or golf is the great leveller. Remember, Vijay had just won the last major of the year the week before, but then sank to 32nd the week in which he had the opportunity to take Tiger's place at the top of the rankings. Tiger, though he did not win, came second and it was one more tournament where he came closer but did not win. Now, he has been winless for quite a long time by his early standards and it's causing him worry. Tiger came up with a classic quote that to now everybody should know why golfers lose hair and get grey fast, but then we opening batsmen can say that too. To the best of my experience, there aren't too many opening batsmen with thick hair, but look around and you will find plenty of fast bowlers with flowing locks even in the mid-fifties of their lives.

But coming back to golf, it certainly has a way to humble a player more than the game of cricket can, and so it probably is a greater leveller than cricket. In golf, one has to be on top of one's game everyday and not just one day, while in cricket, one can get away with a lesser than top effort if the opposition isn't good. The kind of competition that's there in golf does not allow even players like Tiger and Vijay Singh to relax one day, for there are so many snapping at their heels week after week.

One hopes that Vijay, who is refreshingly not intimidated by the West, will one day take up the case of ensuring that there's a major that's played in Asia and Africa

Cricket administrator Jagmohan Dalmiya.

as well. At the moment, with the past major played in USA, there's no major till April next year, which is a long gap and makes one wonder if Asia and Africa who have their summer from September to April should suffer because the authorities aren't prepared to look beyond Western developing countries. There are three majors in USA and one in UK, and with the game getting bigger in Asia, especially in Southeast Asia, there is a case for having a major there. South Africa has a million dollar event, so most of the top golfers go and play there, but they give Asia a miss, unless of course like in Dubai, they get a rich appearance fee. It's something that even the tennis bosses need to look at, for the majors in tennis also finish by the US Open, and there is a lull till the Australian Open in late January. This domination of the West will soon hopefully will come to an end, just as it has in cricket, where, thanks to some bold administrators like Jagmohan Dalmiya, the major events have come to Asia and other developing countries. Other sports could do with administrators with a vision to spread the sport wider around the world and then these sports will truly be global sports.

The Indian cricket team's season hasn't begun in the best possible way, having lost twice to Pakistan whom they beat earlier in the year, and though the major part of the season is still to come, there will be some worried people, but then India has a reputation for being a slow starter and Indian fans will be hoping that they will come good in the Champions Trophy starting a few days later. India has had some injury worries and in a team sport, that's normal and don't forget, they are coming off an off-season and so have taken a bit of time to get going. The matches against England in the Natwest Challenge should be just the tune up they are looking for, but that being said, it's also important to win those games for the confidence to be high for the Champions Trophy. England are certainly on a high after whitewashing the West Indies, and though they have faltered in the limited overs format earlier in the season, right now they will be in a far more confident frame of mind than they were when they took on India last time two years ago.

Andrew Flintoff and Steve Harminson have made enormous progress and England now have a good all-round team, which should be a real challenger for the Champions Trophy, especially as it is being played in England. If they fail to do well, then maybe we can look at whether cricket is a greater leveller than golf, but for the moment, I am convinced that it's golf which is the leveller that sportsmen don't want.

26.08.2004

Solid Side of **SACHIN**

At the end of the first Test at Dhaka, when the ESPN commentators were being polled for their vote for the man of the match award, I nominated myself with my tongue firmly in my cheek. Right throughout the Test, there were so many mentions of Sachin Tendulkar equalling this record or going past that record of mine that I said that with so many regular mentions even when I wasn't playing I should be the man. In the event, it was young Irfan Pathan who won it because he bowled superbly on a pitch that really did not give any assistance to the quicker bowlers, to get 11 wickets in the match and set up a win for India.

Records are of course meant to be overtaken, for therein lies the signs of progress and it also sets up a new benchmark for future generations to follow, so the little champion doing that is great news for Indian cricket. From a personal point of view, if any record, not necessarily mine, but anyone else's too is taken by a deserving player who has been playing consistently well, then there are no twinges at all but if it is taken by a player who was a one off or a flash in the pan then, yes, there would be some shaking of the head. Sachin has been playing for a decade and half and to shoulder the responsibility and to meet the huge expectations of the cricket-mad country that India is, takes a mental fortitude that is not given to many. He has been the backbone of the team for a long-long time and though now his burden is considerably eased with the presence of the classic Dravid, the destructive Sehwag and the elegant Ganguly and Laxman, the opposition is still hunting for his wicket above the others simply because it gives them a psychological boost to go after the others.

When Kapil mentioned that he expects Kumble to get 500 wickets, somebody asked whether it was a realistic target and so also with my expectations of Sachin scoring 50 Test centuries. If both Kaps and I didn't think it was possible we would never have said that. The rate at which Anil is picking wickets means that in three more series he should get to the magic figure. In 2004 with one more Test to be still played (this is being written on the eve of the second Test at Chittagong) Tendulkar has hit three big centuries in what is supposed to be his lean year in Test cricket. With at least six, if not more, years of cricket ahead of him, if he scores three tons a year he will easily get to 50 Test tons and that will take some beating.

Sachin Tendulkar being congratulated by Gavaskar after equaling his record of 34 Test hundreds.

In my first eight years in Tests and in the first 50 Tests, I had 20 centuries. That was a period when the batting wasn't as stable as it was to be in the next eight years as players like Vengsarkar, Jimmy Amarnath, Yashpal Sharma, Sandeep Patil, Mohammad Azharuddin came on to bolster the middle order and there was the incomparable Kapil Dev to follow. Behind him was that fighter Kirmani and later on Kiran More and the bowlers also did not surrender their wicket away as in the earlier time with the likes of Shivlal Yadav, Madan Lal, Roger Binny, Ghavri, Maninder Singh trying their best to stay at the wicket and help build a big total. There was enjoyable opening partnership with Chetan Chauhan, Anshuman Gaekwad, Kris Srikkanth. Ravi Shastri, who began his Test career batting at number 10, went on to open the batting for India, so with the batting looking more solid than in the 1970s it was easier to play a lot more shots than before and obviously, in doing that there were more chances of a dismissal and that is why the consistency of the first eight years was simply not there though the fun in batting was greater because of the freedom to play more shots that the depth in the batting order provided. The fragility of the batting in the 1970s meant that a lot of shots had to be cut out for the risks involved and so batting may have been productive in terms of runs and centuries scored, but it did not really give one too much enjoyment.

Tendulkar, on the other hand, seems to have gone the opposite way for he is more solid now than he was in his first dozen years in International Cricket, and that makes him an even more difficult customer to dismiss as can be seen by the unbeaten big tons that he has been getting. It is this that makes me confident that he will score 50 centuries, if not more, by the time he has had enough of travelling and playing cricket in various parts of the world. Added to his Test tons will also be the One-day centuries and he will be the first to score 100 international centuries which will be truly phenomenal and well nigh impossible to beat.

Nothing is certain in this game of glorious uncertainties but whatever Tendulkar finishes up with in terms of runs, centuries, appearances in Tests and ODIs, will be hard to achieve unless someone as prodigiously talented comes on the scene and starts playing international cricket at the same age or earlier than when the little champion began his journey on the road to fame and glory.

It's been wonderful to have seen the beginning of that journey and the way he has handled the ups and the very few downs and kept his focus on doing his best for India. He has still some way to go and there is not the slightest doubt that he will continue striving for India, bear unflinchingly and uncomplainingly all the pain that a sporting career brings and continue to delight his admirers all over the world for a lot more time. And yes, while he will beat all existing records there's one record of mine that he won't beat for sure.

This is the 500th fortnightly column which began in 1985 and am pretty certain that the little champion will let the old man enjoy this record forever. Thank you dear readers and thank you all those who take this column for making it such an enthralling experience.

16.12.2004

TSUNAMI of Cricket

F irst and foremost, heartfelt condolences to all those who were affected by the tsunami. It brought into sharp perspective that sport is nothing compared to what nature can unleash and how helpless man is when nature's fury strikes. Hopefully, the cricketing world will go out of its way to help those affected and help in their time of need. Sri Lanka have called off their tour of NewZealand, not only because of the damage done to their country, but also because some of the players' relatives were affected badly by the tsunami after-effects. In such a scenario, it's difficult to play cricket or any other sport for that matter and the mind simply cannot concentrate.

In cricketing terms, the tsunami is the Australian team, as it sweeps all teams that face up to it, whether in Australia or away. The manner in which they have beaten Pakistan in the second Test, after at one stage looking in real trouble, tells you why they are such a superior side to the others playing world cricket. The resurgent England side is probably the only team that can give them a run for their money, and that series promises to be a real corker in the coming year. England too have shown remarkable resilience in coming back from the dead, so to speak, and apart from a couple of changes, they too will be the side to watch out for over the next few years.

The other teams seem to have problems galore and not necessarily on the field, but off it too, as can be seen with what's happening in the West Indies. Though they seem to have settled their differences with their board, it is not the best way to prepare for a tour, especially that of Australia. To do well in Australia, there must not be any thoughts other than playing cricket, and hopefully the Windies will now put all other issues behind and go to Australia with a determination to show that their win in the ICC Champions Trophy wasn't a fluke. There will be lots of interest in their tour, because they are being coached by an Australian, and how they respond to him will be the key. In recent times, a lot of the young West Indies players have shown scant regard for authority and acted more like spoilt brats than highly paid performers. For those of us who have been great supporters and followers of Windies cricket, their downfall has been painful, and to see them win the Champions Trophy has kindled hopes that they could be on the comeback trail to glory. Though they

Gundappa Vishwanath during his power play.

will be playing in Australia in limited-overs matches, it will at least show how much progress they have made, especially in terms of temperament.

Pakistan's show in the second Test was a much more improved one than the one in Perth, but then not too many teams prosper on the fast bouncy pitches of Perth, and feel a lot better when they play at other venues, where though there will be bounce it won't be the steepling kind as in Perth. Pakistan had the firepower in Akhtar and if only the much-rated but under-performing Sami had bowled well, then the Australians who were reeling would have been in more trouble. It was left to hometown boy Justin Langer to play an incredible knock to take the game away from Pakistan, and the lack of support bowlers shows why other teams pale in comparison to the Aussies. Most people think it's the Aussie batting that gets them out of tough situations, and if a team has someone of the calibre of Adam Gilchrist batting at number seven, there is not much to worry even if half the side is back in the pavilion with not too many runs on the board. However, it's the Aussie variety in bowling that wins them the matches. There is just no weak link there and so there is no escaping to one end, where there can be some relief. The Aussie spirit of not giving up is another reason why they can dig themselves out of a hole. The manner in which Jason Gillespie has developed his batting is a prime example of Aussie spirit. He is well aware that there is Brett Lee breathing down his and Kasprowicz's neck for a place in the playing eleven, so he makes sure that he has another string to his bow. If India's bowlers who are all pretty handy with the bat can emulate Gillespie's grit and commonsense approach to batting, there will be more runs for the Indians in every game that they play. Unfortunately, because the Indian batting line-up is so highly rated and rightly so, the bowlers tend to think that if the batsmen haven't done it, then how can they do what the batsmen could not? If only our bowlers who find opposition tail-enders not giving their wickets away easily were to follow that and not gift their wickets away, then India would have less to worry about.

Speaking of the tail not wagging too much takes me back to my last column, where many pointed out that I had overlooked G.R. Vishwanath. No, I hadn't, for Vishy was the one batsman in my first eight years who took the opposition apart and scored runs when they were badly needed, but with no disrespect to the others who batted in those first eight years, apart from Vishy, there were no other reliable players and that's why when in the next eight years the others came along, it was easier to play a few more shots than in the first eight years, when the responsibility was on Vishy and myself more than the others. Since I was emphasising the second eight years rather than the first, Vishy's name was not taken for he was barely there for two of the last eight years. How can I forget the one man who to me was the best batsman of my generation and who when he scored a century for India, meant that India either won the game or drew it, but never lost it. Thank you, dear readers for your observation, and you know more than anyone else that if there was Vishy in the Indian side, there would be far more artistry to enjoy on the field, and even more fun in the dressing room.

30.12.2004

*... legend Sir
... Roberts, English
... spinner Norman
... South African
... Shaun Pollock
... African pacer
... Ackermann and
... man Len Hutton.*

THE WORLD OF
Bonding and Camaraderie

L
ooking at the tremendous way the ICC World team has gelled and is having a great time in the few days that they have been together, brings back memories of my tour to Australia as a member of the Rest of the World side in 1971-72. It was the happiest of my tours, for in spite of it being my first year in International Cricket and the presence of some really big names in the game then, like the Captain Garry Sobers and Rohan Kanhai, to name just two, it was a trip full of great fun. The Sunday club, which I then tried to make a part of an Indian team when I became captain, was first seen on the Rest of the World trip in 1971. It was the brain child of Norman Gifford and it became an evening where players let their hair down—and in those days most had plenty of hair—and it helped not only to bring the players together but also removed any barriers there may have been between seniors and juniors in the team. There were, apart from Gifford, some other really funny guys on the team like Richard Hutton, son of the famous Len Hutton and with him going on in his typical British dry humour a quip was never too far away. It was also the time when India and Pakistan went to war and yet there was hardly any tension between the Indian players and Pakistani players in the team. If anything, the one abiding memory is that of the team Vice Captain Intikhab Alam making sure that any chits passed on to him by the owner of a Pakistani restaurant which we used to frequent, being torn off unopened. Those chits contained notes on what was happening in the war from whatever the restaurant owner was gleaning from the radio, which we weren't able to access at all. That mate-ship and camaraderie is still there and it's always a pleasure to meet up with any of that team even after all these years. It was the only opportunity for someone like Hylton Ackerman and the Pollock brothers to show their talent to the world, for South Africa was ostracised by the sporting world by then, for their reprehensive apartheid policy.

The other memorable tours that I have been a part of were the 1977-78 Indian tour of Australia under Bishan Singh Bedi. The captain himself was always game for a laugh and so it was easy to have the guys coming up with a joke a day. The funny guys in that team were Ashok Mankad, Madan Lal and of course G.R. Vishwanath who would quietly say something that would bring the house down.

Englishman Len Hutton.

The manager of the team, Polly Umrigar, had a hard time to get the guys to be serious, though of course when the game was on, everybody was dead serious playing for India. The 1980-81 tour to Australia was also great fun with the Sunday club being introduced again after a gap and Sandeep Patil with his henchman, Karsan Ghavri and with permanent bartender, Bharath Reddy, the club meetings were sometimes rowdy but always side-splitting. With more media presence beginning in the early 1980s, these Sunday clubs stopped altogether and I believe that it has taken away a great part of team bonding that is so essential when one is away from one's country. Then the 1987 world team that played in the MCC bicentenary game also was an enjoyable tour though it was only for three weeks or so. By that time, there was a bit of sledging in cricket and so guys who had slagged off each other were a bit wary of each other but by the end of the tour were friends and realised that not all the sledgers were bad after all.

In this present team, there is Muralitharan and Chris Gayle who are naturally funny and with Makhaya Ntini coming up with his own brand of humour, there's plenty of laughter around. Flintoff brings the British humour, which is understated and there's hardly any hang-ups in the team, which has some of the biggest names in world cricket today. The bonding has been terrific and credit must go to the manager, Goolam Rajah as well as the coach and the skipper, Shaun Pollock who has a mischievous streak in him too. Obviously, winning makes a big difference and if the world team manages to come back and win the One-day series then it will mean more jokes and more laughs in the dressing room and team meetings. As this is being written, the world team are one down with two to go and the players playing in the Super Test will be joining the team for the second One-dayer, so there could be some more funny men there too.

The World team concept is a good one, for there's no doubt it makes for better understanding of different temperaments and different cricketing cultures and when these players go back to play for their countries, they will tell their teammates that some of the players help to break down barriers between the seniors, and puts the juniors and put the newcomers at ease a lot faster than otherwise.

07.10.2005

PENSION and Less Tension!

'Well done' is the only way to react to the news that the Finance Committee of the BCCI has decided to pay a monthly pension to India's former cricketers. The heartening part is that it's not just Test cricketers but also those who have only played First-class cricket in India who will be eligible. There has been a committee formed to look at what should be the criteria for qualifying to get the pension, for it's understandable that playing just one First-class game would not qualify for the pension, for then there would be an unbelievable financial burden on the BCCI. One wishes that the BCCI had taken a former cricketer like Polly Umrigar on the committee to decide the cut-off point, be it the number of First-class matches or years as a First-class cricketer. May be even someone like Anand Shukla who did not get to play for India, but was a remarkable performer at the First-class level. Of course, one of the committee men, M.P. Pandove, the joint secretary, has represented Punjab for a number of years and would be able to put the First-class players' view to the BCCI.

Previously, the BCCI had started a pension scheme for retired Test players who are getting Rs 5000/- per month with the cut-off being those who got the India cap at least five times (five Tests). Today, the India cap has lost its value, with even the support staff wearing it, but that's a topic for another time and not in the middle of an important series like the one against Pakistan. But it will be fantastic if the marketing committee of the BCCI takes a decision on the logo on the replica apparel that will be merchandised to fans and supporters. If one looks at the replica clothing for Cricket Australia, one will notice that the Kangaroo and the Emu that are there on the players' clothing is not there for the fans while in all other aspects, the coloured clothing is exactly like what the players wear. When one starts playing at the school level, the dream is to get the India cap. Unfortunately, today that cap can be bought at the nearest street corner and this is an aspect that the marketing committee must give serious thought to before making team merchandise available to fans.

The other aspect that the BCCI needs to be congratulated on is for the decision to advance the Ranji Trophy final by one day, so that two of Uttar Pradesh's players picked for the India Under-19 World Cup team are able to play in the finals and

then go to Sri Lanka for the Junior World Cup. The Ranji Trophy final is the biggest domestic game in the calendar and it should be played with the best of players available, barring injury and national duty of course. So it will be played between a full-strength Uttar Pradesh team and Bengal and though it clashes with the third Test in Karachi, there will still be plenty of interest in it. Hopefully, the BCCI has already invited a chief guest to give away the Ranji Trophy and not like last year when the coach of the losing team gave away the trophy to the winners. It would be fantastic for the winning team to receive the trophy from the BCCI president himself and if he is not available due to prior commitments, if a former great like Kapil Dev were to give it to the winners. These are moments to cherish and so, to top the victory by getting the prize from a big personality is the icing on the cake.

26.01.2006

GREG AND LARA Show

India's loss to the West Indies and that too by the big margin of 4-1 has created consternation among Indian fans, who expected the result to be the other way around. Certainly after the manner in which Dravid guided the team to a victory in the first match of the series, Indian supporters expected that the West Indians would cave in and lose the series. That it didn't happen has meant that some sections of the electronic media have gone into overdrive as far as the blame game is concerned and the favourite whipping boys have predictably been Greg Chappell, Kiran More and the skipper, Rahul Dravid. With the massive publicity and hype that surrounded the appointment of Greg Chappell as the coach of the Indian team, his every move has been scrutinised, and debated and discussed threadbare and there has been no shortage of opinions on his performance as the coach. When India was winning, all the credit was given to him and now when India hasn't done too well, the blame also is being laid at his door. If the players thus felt deprived of their share of the glory when India won, they are very thankful now that they are escaping the blame as fingers are being pointed at the coach. Even Brian Lara, the West Indies captain, has gone on record as saying Chappell's remark being the catalyst to the improved performance by the West Indian team. Lara in fact called it a 'sly remark' and cleverly used it as a motivating factor for the West Indians. What Lara has also done with that observation is to create a doubt about Chappell in the minds of the Indian supporters in much the same way as Chappell tried to create a mental block in the West Indian players by suggesting that they had forgotten how to win.

In the mind games that are pretty much a part of international sport, there is always a chance that a remark might boomerang but Chappell did nothing wrong in his comment, which was well timed after India won the first game with just a ball to spare. At that stage there was every chance that the West Indians would lapse back into their wayward, wasteful ways after having beaten a depleted Zimbabwe side a few days earlier but that it did not happen was entirely due to Brian Lara. In his third 'avataar' as captain, Lara has been nothing short of brilliant and the manner in which he has utilised the resources at his disposal, has been truly masterly. In his previous editions as captain, nobody would have credited Lara with

Indian all-rounder Irfan Pathan.

being one of the better captains in the game but this, his third and final innings, certainly looks good to change the perception of him as a leader of men. That his team won in such a comprehensive manner and without a century contribution from him, tells how much he has made the players believe in their own ability and the confidence he has given them. Luckily, in the West Indies, there is not much hype about the coach, so the West Indian coach has not been given the credit for the team's performance on the field and there's little doubt that the return of Lara at the helm has turned the tide for the West Indians at least in the limited overs format of the game.

There are some in India who are suggesting that lack of experience in the team caused them to stumble and while that may have been true of the bowling, it wasn't that department that cost India the series but the batting and there was no shortage of experience there. If anything, there was shortage of competition and a confusion about the roles that could have led to such a dismal batting performances. When a team has a player who struggles to accelerate in the 'A' team matches as a reserve, then how can the players be worried about being replaced by him? When a team includes a player woefully short of runs and that player takes his own sweet time to get runs then the team is bound to be short of runs in the final analysis. While some players get all the opportunities, some others do not even get a whiff of a chance to show their mettle and that creates complacency. If in the event of injury the reserve player comes in, then realises it's his only chance, there's no wonder if he is thinking more about himself than the team. The players also did not seem to be aware of the specific role they had to play. Pathan's promotion to the number three spot can work as a surprise move to throw off the opposition bowlers but he has seldom scored at the rate he should be for that is the purpose of sending him up the order. What is forgotten is that it is far harder for regular batsmen to play the unorthodox shots in the final surge for runs, so they are actually better off at the start of the innings where they can play in the natural way they are accustomed to than coming in to bat in the final overs and trying to throw their bats at everything. It was this confusion about their roles that did not help anybody as Pathan tried to bat like a batsman and the batsmen tried to slog like bowlers.

Just imagine if the roles of the coach and the support staff were exchanged. While there's little doubt that the coach would not do a bad job as a physical trainer since as a former player he would have trained a fair bit, it would be impossible for the physical conditioning expert to be a coach. Similarly if the biomechanist—oops! he is a sports scientist now and before that called himself assistant manager, assistant coach on previous tours—were to swap places with the physiotherapist, would it work? But then 'all-rounders' like him have seldom been seen in cricket before.

02.06.2006

GET SMARTER, BCCI

A lot of discussions have started at the decision of the Indian team's physical trainer to take the Indian squad out of the Bangalore city limits to a training facility where they will be able to train and work without any outside distraction. The TV channels and the papers have been full of speculation as to what exactly the players will be doing. There's talk of the team doing rock climbing, boating and God knows what else. Of course only an Indian cricket squad will get everybody up feverishly at the kind of training methods used to get it into top condition. These methods have been tried before by other teams but apart from the Australians, nobody has kept up a winning streak. While we should all look at different methods tried with an open mind, as to the usefulness for getting the players into top physical shape when the talk is about getting the players to bond is a bit naive. I mean if the players who have been pretty much together as a team for years now, with the odd dropout and the odd newcomer in, has not bonded by now, then they never will. Still it will be interesting to see how the whole exercise adds up and if it helps the players, then great.

More than the various exercise and training options that the team is undergoing, it is important to know who makes the call on these and also who makes the decision on when a training camp should start or how long it should be. Is it a decision of the selectors or just one selector? Is it a decision of the support staff and again just one member of the support staff? Is it a decision of the coach? Or the captain? Or the BCCI president? Or the BCCI secretary? Or the BCCI Working Committee?

The reason these questions are necessary is because it is important to know who decides the optimum length of a training session. Who decides that physical conditioning should take precedence over cricket skills training? And also who decides that the players after their physical training can go back home for a break and then come back for the cricket skills camp? The BCCI is a rich body but surely it is a total waste of public money that players do all the rock climbing, etc., and then undergo the travails of waiting for rain-delayed flights at various airports and go home for two days and then travel all the way back to Bangalore. It is certainly not a bright idea to go home just for two days and then come back to the same place again. They may as well stay in Bangalore where without the pressure of the

One of the Indian greats, Rahul Dravid.

team curfews, there is likelihood of a greater bonding than in the intensity of the physical conditioning camp where each player will be looking to complete the task given to him. The gap may be because the coach is coming back after a well-deserved holiday but then the physical conditioning camp could have started a few days later and thus saved the player the trouble of travelling back and forth. Those who have had to endure long waits at airports know how stressful it can be and that's why it could have been a good idea to have kept the boys in Bangalore, given them a couple of days or longer break and then start the cricket specific camp. And don't forget the lakhs it would have saved for the BCCI in air ticket expenses.

And pray, tell me, what is going to happen to those guys who are unable to cope with the new methods of rock climbing, etc.? Apart from being the butt of some good-natured leg-pulling by teammates, is anything going to happen to them? Some of them may not be able to do any of the new training exercises but are absolutely brilliant in their respective cricketing discipline of batting and bowling. So, are they going to be dropped because they couldn't climb a rock? That's unthinkable, isn't it? Every player is different and has different methods of coping with the physical demands of the sport. A standard training method does not always work.

From personal experience I know that I could never do laps of the ground like some others could and so I had decided on my own methods to meet the demands of international cricket. To have played sixteen years without missing too many matches with muscular injuries, does say that it wasn't entirely wrong. Fortunately, the trainers then—though disapproving at first—were understanding and realised that I wasn't shirking but simply unable to do it because of physical limitations and that I was compensating by doing my other exercises. In the current scenario, there will be more than one certainty who will be unable to meet the training requirements. Mind you, this is not only about the special training methods being tried out but even normal training methods where these certainties struggle to do what some other younger players do with ease but that in any way does not take anything away from their cricketing capabilities. One thing is for definite, that among the seniors the skipper Rahul Dravid will be the first to do all that is asked of him, for among the seniors he is the fittest of the lot and has observed the fitness regime throughout his career and is thus able to meet the extra demands that the team makes of him.

That's why he is able to not only bat for hours but also keep wickets when the team needs it. Talk about leading from the front. That's Rahul Dravid for you.

27.07.2006

One and Only **AGASSI**

ndre Agassi's farewell address to the crowd that had come to cheer him showed why he was such a popular player not just with the paying public but with the media as well as fellow players. Andy Roddick has gone on record to say how Agassi would ring him and offer advice on how to play certain opponents. In the cut-throat world of modern sport, such gestures are unheard of. No wonder he got a standing ovation when he returned to the locker room after his loss to Benjamin Becker. Agassi's career thus finished with a loss to a famous last name though the first name wasn't Boris but Benjamin. When he came to the media room later it was this ovation that was still ringing in his ears and it must have been the sweetest sound of music that a player hears. No matter what the crowd feels, no matter what TV commentators, former players or the media feel, it is the locker room recognition that a player craves for. It is these fellow pros who know what it takes to go out there and gut it out when things are not working. It is the fellow players who know of the hard work and effort that has been put in to get into that physical and mental condition. It is they who know of the pressures and tensions that a player undergoes and it is because of this that recognition and respect from the dressing room towers above any other, be it National Awards, public applause or praise from former players. In a team sport it becomes even more important, for, when you are pulling for the team the rest of the guys know it and understand and thus recognise it. Today when you see a batsman acknowledge the applause for a half century or a century, the first thing he does is to raise his bat to the dressing room and then to the rest of the crowd though there are some who don't even recognise the crowd's cheers after getting the salute from the dressing room.

Agassi was sought after by the media because he had the enviable knack of saying something profoundly different and so was an interviewer's delight. Even when the Sampras-Agassi rivalry was at its peak, the media gave more prominence to Agassi simply because he had a different take on what was after all another tennis match between him and Sampras. The latter won almost twice the number of majors that Agassi won but still did not get the media that his feats deserved. Sampras talked clinically while Agassi spoke passionately and so was invariably quote-worthy. He was a bit theatrical too in the way he blew kisses to all four

The flamboyant Andre Agassi.

corners of the court after winning his match and he did that after his loss in the U.S. Open which was one of the rare occasions that he did so after losing. This rapport with the crowd was something that other players have craved for but not always got, especially in New York at the U.S. Open.

Agassi had announced his intention to retire after the U.S. Open and so all his matches were sell-outs and the crowds came to have one last glimpse of a player who had brought a new dimension to tennis not just with his play but also with his attire, his behaviour and his interaction with other stake-holders of the sport. What is praiseworthy is the manner in which he has used his stature in the game to raise funds for his Andre Agassi Foundation that helps underprivileged children get a proper education and vocational guidance in his native Las Vegas. Agassi, the tennis player, will go down in history as one of its greatest exponents and entertainer but the legacy that his humanitarian work will leave behind is going to be far more important than his tennis deeds.

Speaking of farewells, even as Agassi has got a grand one not just from the crowds, but also from the media and fellow players, no such luck for Pakistan's captain Inzamam-ul Haq in England. That should not come as a surprise considering the kind of frosty relations that are the norm for Pakistan – England cricketing encounters. If it had been an Australian player, you can be sure that at every Test on international ground, he would have been applauded all the way to the crease and then off it as well, for apart from the cricketing rivalry with Australia being more than a century old there is an awe about the Aussies that the Brits feel. Yes, Viv Richards has had that kind of farewell as did those two magnificent bowlers Courtney Walsh and Curtly Ambrose but don't forget they also played County cricket for a number of years and so had in their own way made a contribution to English cricket. Not that Indians should complain about farewells, for leave aside applause, they get booed when they fail and so would be quite happy if they got no applause so long as they didn't get any boos either.

It is not about Inzamam not getting a decent farewell; it's just about the indifference that the English feel towards players from the subcontinent, however great they may be. Inzamam's deeds in both Test and One-day cricket are gigantic by any standards and he is one of the greats of the game but maybe his mild-mannered persona and not being media savvy has meant he won't get the kind of farewell that players from Australia would get in England. Shane Warne got a wonderful send off though it was dimmed to an extent by the joy that the crowd felt on England regaining the Ashes after a long time. Maybe that's why the leggie hasn't ruled out another trip to England in 2009. Mind you, he knows there's bagful of wickets on offer when he bowls to Englishmen.

The ICC Champions Trophy in India will offer Indian cricket lovers a final look at many cricketing greats who may never visit Indian shores as cricketers again and it also provides them with a wonderful opportunity to give these stars a memorable send-off. Hopefully it will be with cheers that will bring back fond memories of their visits to India rather than the boos, which do nothing more than diminish all of us in the eyes of the world.

07.09.2006

DADA of a Gesture

When Australia were nine wickets down in the second innings at Nagpur, Mahendra Singh Dhoni, the skipper of the Indian team, asked Sourav Ganguly to take the reins of the captaincy. Ganguly was playing his last Test match and it was his final day, and by giving him the charge of the team for the final wicket, Dhoni was acknowledging the huge role Ganguly had played in taking Indian cricket forward with his captaincy. This gesture, as well as the one at the end of the previous Test at Delhi, where he carried Anil Kumble on his shoulders along with other players showed Dhoni's respect and regard for the seniors in the team.

The seniors had served Indian cricket with distinction and they needed to be given a warm send-off and the skipper did that; and in doing so, won even more fans than he already has. In Indian culture, respect for the seniors is ingrained right from early age, and though it can be taken to an extreme when even teenagers not related to each other are referred to as 'uncle' or 'aunty', it is still something to be admired in an age when being irreverent and having an attitude is the theme of the season. Of course, respect does not mean that if the seniors have to be left out of the side it shouldn't be done, but giving them time to do it on their own rather than having them face the ignominy of being omitted after such a long illustrious career and service to the game, would be the right thing to do.

The baton has passed in to the right hands indeed and in Dhoni, India has a captain who will not be cowed down by the reputation of the opposition nor be worried about what his position would be if India does not do well. He did show that he was confident about his own place in the team by opting out of the Test series against Sri Lanka and taking a much needed rest after a real hectic season, and don't forget, as the wicket keeper, he has a lot more of a workload than others. The players who took his place hardly used the chances given and if anything, they have ensured that there is no option but Dhoni as wicket keeper for the Indian team.

Under Dhoni, the team has taken the fight to the opposition but in an acceptable way. They have played an attacking, aggressive brand of cricket and have refused to take a backward step even in tough situations. In many respects, they have learnt the good aspects of Australian cricket where no game is won or lost till the last ball

Anil Kumble and his teammates after the Delhi Test, where he announced his retirement from all forms of cricket.

is bowled and no effort spared while wearing the country's cap. The bowlers have also picked up the Australian way of not making a drama if their teammate misses a catch or misfields and walk back to the bowling mark to bowl the next ball. There is no point in further embarrassing a fielder who is already feeling terrible after missing a catch or misfielding. If anything, any drama makes the fielder feel resentful and might make him ask if bowlers never bowl a bad ball at all.

Hopefully, they will never pick up the Australian tactic of mental disintegration of the opposition by abuse of the viliest kind, though there is some evidence that India too has given back in ample measure in the recent series. 'Sledging' is more effective if it's done with humour and sarcasm for then the player at whom it is directed tends to think about it. Abuse invariably leads to the player getting more determined to show that it doesn't affect him and so it can backfire. There is also the danger of there being a bit of violence since it is personal and insulting. That kind of language will invite a physical retort anywhere else, so why should it be a surprise if there's a shove on the field? That's pretty much a mild reaction to the abuse the player has received. Unless the umpires are tough and don't look the other way, this will continue since Australian cricket is in denial about its players' language on the field. Sure, it is not tiddlywinks as we are often reminded but was it tiddlywinks when Bradman, Benaud and Simpson were playing? If there was no need felt to use that kind of language then and still win Test matches, why is it felt necessary to do so now?

It would be far more effective to have the kind of sledging that India did where the Aussies were told especially during the Mohali Test 'guru has destroyed our cricket, now he is doing that to yours' certainly there is no doubt that 'guru's' face in the Australian dressing room was just the incentive the Indians needed to lift their game a notch or two above the usual.

The Australians came with a pretty large supporting staff and here the Australian media is not being counted but they did not feel the need for a 'biomechanist' nor did 'guru' insist on one, as was done with the Indian cricket Board. Of course, any designation would have done just to have ones mate around in this 'silly, backward, frustrating' country of ours and the authorities in their awe were only too willing to accommodate and some are still doing it. The Australian Board wouldn't, because it knows more about who is a real biomechanist and who is just one in name.

India has begun well with a thumping win in the first One-dayer against England and if they keep it up they will certainly be on the fast track to being the number one team in the world in the other two forms of the game. Don't forget that they are the world champs in the T20 format of the game.

14.11.2008

...mbai terror ...Taj hotel; New ...spot for Yuvraj ...ngland skipper ...etersen coming ...hotel amid ...rity.

Bless You, **KP**

No praise can be too high for the brave decision of the England team to resume their tour of India after the traumatic happenings in Mumbai. The England and Wales Cricket Board also deserves credit for allowing the players to take their own decision, without putting any pressure on them. In the end, the statement of England skipper Kevin Pietersen that 'they are ready to stand shoulder to shoulder with India in this hour', has gone down extremely well in a country that has been hurt beyond belief, and given it the confidence that they will not be alone in fighting this scourge which is bigger and greater than any illness or ailment that mankind knows.

As with anything, there will be the cynics who will sneer and suggest that this decision was prompted by the lure of the Indian Premier League, but then the IPL had a very successful first season with just one English player, and the absence of English players in the second one won't make too much of a difference. In any case, there are probably a handful of English players who the franchisers would be interested in, and that leaves us with a majority who wouldn't get a glance their way, and they could have voted to withdraw from the tour. Instead, they and the coaching and support staff, who the franchisers weren't interested in, voted for the tour to go ahead. That the decision was unanimous tells you that England is indeed committed to stand with India and this gesture of theirs will generate more goodwill in a cricket-mad country than any diplomatic or political stand.

If, as some have suggested, it was money that made England come back, then the question can be turned around to ask these objectors, if it was a lack of an invitation to be part of the IPL that is making them feel this way.

When the suicide bombings took place in London in 2005 there was nearly a suggestion that cricket should be stopped, and Australia should go home; so why should it be different this time around? Even if one takes into account the normal mourning period in India after a death, that also had passed when the Chennai Test match began, so those raising objections could be having another motive and the old saying of three fingers pointing back at the pointer holds true.

What the events of 26 November have shown is that cricket is but a trivial pursuit, and there is more to life than a game of sport, but as with anything life

The Taj on fire: the days of the Mumbai terror attacks.

moves on and while sympathising with all those who lost their near and dear ones, the decision of the England team needs to be applauded and not criticised. The irony is that those who are criticising the tour resuming are not shy of earning money commenting and writing about the tour. If they were genuine about their objections, then they should have the courage not to comment about this tour, and earn money from an exercise that they feel shouldn't be taking place. How hypocritical is that? But putting money where their mouths are is never easy as we all know to comment is easy but action is not.

India have chosen Yuvraj to replace Sourav Ganguly, and that is no surprise after his terrific batting in the One-dayers against the same English team. It is a wonderful chance for him to cement a place in the Test team, for with his fielding and occasional bowling he is a big plus even before he faces a single ball with the bat. What is still hard to understand is the stubbornness with which Indian selectors are not releasing the reserve players to go and play in the Ranji Trophy matches once the final eleven is selected. Sure, keep two players in the reserves but release the other two so that they are in match trim. Unfortunately, even the reserves seem to have a negative mindset where they worry that if they fail in the Ranji game, then they won't be selected for the next Test, when in fact they should be looking at the prospect of playing the Ranji to enhance their chances of getting a place in the Test eleven. If they are not confident of doing well in a Ranji game, then how are they expected to do so in a Test match?

There was a feeling in the past that the Indian team had become like a cozy club, but it's to be hoped that under Mahendra Singh Dhoni and the chairmanship of Kris Srikkanth, that this won't be the case and players will have to consistently deliver to be wearing the India colours.

The next few days will tell us what Indian cricket has in store, and if the Champions League has been rescheduled or not, but till then let us watch the current series to see if India can maintain the intensity that they showed against Australia and win the series, and go to the number two spot in the Test rankings.

12.12.2008

NO DRESSING ROOM is Perfect

The resignation of Kevin Pietersen from the England captaincy and the sacking of the coach Peter Moores, has all been too bizarre to understand. Sure we are miles away from the action, so will probably never know the full story, but where and how it started is also a mystery. Pietersen was on a holiday in Africa when the issue boiled up, and before he could return, he had to resign and the coach lost his job. There was nothing in the public domain said by both persons, so how it all came to such a pass is baffling. Be that as it may, what has been interesting, is to read British papers and to see the extent of the divisions in the English dressing room. If it brings a wry smile on the faces of those in the subcontinent, don't be surprised, because for years the Brit media has gone to town about the friction in the dressing rooms of the teams of the subcontinent, and making believe that there were none in their own rooms.

The fact is that there is no team including the Australians in their pomp where there was not some friction in the dressing room. It is virtually impossible not to have a tension-free dressing room, for the pressures of international sport are such that there are always some temperaments that are fragile, and so in need of monitoring and assuaging. The sound bytes in the public domain will always be about the harmony and spirit in the dressing room, but make no mistake; underneath it all there is bound to be some disappointment.

How teams manage to leave that behind in the dressing room, and go out and put their best foot forward on the field is what makes that team win. Have you ever heard of a present skipper and coach ever being criticised by other team members in public? No, simply because the players, however good they are, know that their future depends on the coach and the captain, and so will sing hosannas about them in public, even though they may not always agree with them about everything. The moment the skipper and the coach are out of the job, the knives come out and the disaffected get their voice back, but will make sure that the present occupants will not be criticised.

By all accounts, the difference between Moores and Pietersen were about selection and training methods, and Pietersen wanted somebody who could lift the team out of its under-achieving status, to those performing brilliantly in all games.

Kerry Packer, whose idea changed ODI cricket.

In a team sport, all players will never be successful and there will always be some who are not major contributors to a win, but the manner in which these non-performers help the team achieve its overall objective, is what makes a good team.

It is becoming increasingly clear that including the skipper and coach in the selection meeting causes more problems, especially when they do not get the players that they feel are necessary for their plans.

The Australians have never had the skipper and the coach in the selection meetings, though of course, the selectors will talk and find out from the duo as to what they are looking for. Here it is not individual names that they are looking for, but positions that they feel need to be looked at, for example, an all-rounder or a leg spinner or a left-arm seamer. Then it is up to the selectors to go out and find the blokes that fit in with what the skipper and the coach want. This way the captain and the coach are given the players and told to show how good they are by winning with the resources given to them. The plus with this system is that the skipper and the coach don't get blamed for getting their favourites in the team. Over a period of time, the dressing room becomes settled with some players, and when they are in bad form there is a reluctance to leave out some and bring in new faces because there is the uncertainty of how the dressing room atmosphere will be affected.

If anything, how the new player's inclusion will affect the performances on the field should be the only criteria and how much value he brings on the field, and the balance he adds to the team should be the only issues to consider.

In any case, it was only a matter of time before Pietersen was going to be given the push because the establishment has never been too sure of him. Why, one former skipper has even said that he was a foreign captain since Pietersen comes from South Africa. Remember the Kerry Packer times when Tony Greig, another South-African born and bred player was England captain. When the story broke out that he was part of the recruiting team for Kerry Packer, most of the English media went to town about his South African upbringing and suggesting that since he was not English-born and bred, it was to be expected. If England was a totally crime-free society, then such a sentiment would have been understood, but it was laughable then and laughable now that where a player was born should determine his integrity and honesty.

Well, Pietersen born in South Africa is gone and Andrew Strauss who too has some links there has taken over as the England captain for the West Indies tour. English cricket is in turmoil and there is widespread chest beating about how all this is going to affect the Ashes clash later in the year. But hey guys, you lost badly to India, so how about defeating West Indies first?

09.01.2009

BCCI, the Eternal Target

Engl and has landed in the West Indies after upsetting a few passengers who did not know when they booked the flight that there would be an unscheduled stop in St Kitts to allow the England cricket team to disembark. As a compensation, the passengers were given England cricket team cufflinks and some other memento but as some remarked, they would rather get to their destinations in time than get cufflinks, and pray what to do with cufflinks if you are a woman. Be that as it may, just imagine the headlines, especially in the overseas papers, if it was the Indian cricket team for whom a flight was diverted with an unscheduled stop. There would have been stories of how BCCI is using its money power to change flight paths, how Lalit Modi (who seems to be their favourite target) got the pilot to change course and fly at a higher altitude , how some BCCI official got a first class seat even if he had actually bought one—of course, all with that most useful word, 'allegedly' added before all the allegations as is usually done with speculative stories. Right now the latest allegation is BCCI using its might to get a One-dayer taken away from Dambulla because it does not have facilities for a day-night game and the agreements between the Boards say that there must be four day-night games. Now if there is a written agreement that there should be four day-nighters and if the ground does not have lights then how is the BCCI to be blamed if the Sri Lankan Board has taken the game away and in any case, isn't the itinerary announced only after all these things are sorted out, and therefore it is sensible not to go by the tentative itinerary that is usually given out.

Just before the England team left for the Caribbean, there was a conclave convened by the England and Wales Cricket Board which was attended by some former England skippers and chairmen of the Counties as well as members of the England team. It was a high-powered meeting to look at ways and means to take the game forward and such exercises are very good if those attending it are honest in their assessments and views about the state of the game and what needs urgent attention. The BCCI carried out such an exercise with its administrators and seven former captains immediately after the exit of the Indian team in 2007 from the World Cup, and some, if not all, the suggestions made then have been taken on Board and implemented which does encourage other such exchanges in future.

The IPL Man: Lalit Modi.

One of the ideas that seemed to have come out of the conclave in England, is to have internationals between other countries in England, say between India and Pakistan which will draw huge support from the expatriates living in England or in nearby Europe. The hitch may well be in revenue sharing with the other Boards because, if those Boards are not going to get the lion's share, they will simply not agree to have these matches as it will take away from the matches between the countries when they play due to a possibility of overkill. The ECB is not ready as yet to accept revenue sharing for such games and that could make it a non-starter. The fact is that other countries won't get invited because it is not commercially viable, so New Zealand and West Indies playing in England will not get the same kind of commercial support that India playing Pakistan or Australia will get. So, it will be a case of trying to exploit India's commercial power, and while the relations between the two Boards have improved considerably after the recent Test series and especially after ECB encouraged their team to return after the Mumbai attacks, the Indian administrators of today are no longer going to fall for the prospect of an invitation to the MCC President's box for the Test at Lord's cricket ground and sign away Indian cricket's commercial rights just like that.

Some former England cricketers have demanded that the BCCI share its profits from the Indian Premier League with the other Boards that allow its players to participate, forgetting that the IPL is a domestic tournament and if that criteria is to be adopted then the ECB, Cricket Australia and other Boards where overseas players play County or Shield Cricket should also be splitting revenues with the other Boards. Most of these former players nurse a grouse because they have not been invited to be part of the commentary team or be connected with the IPL in some way, that's all.

Last year, at this time, there was excitement all over the cricketing world when the player auction for the IPL franchises was to take place. There were many big-name players who felt deflated when they heard the price at which they were bought and especially after seeing that some players, not even regulars in the India teams, were bought for much more. Australia were the world champs then and its players understandably thought that they would be millionaire players in the IPL but apart from Andrew Symonds, none of them got even half that amount, so naturally not just disappointment but some resentment also grew. After the shenanigans of that season in Australia, the Australian players' marketability as endorsers of products also went down as Indian companies reassessed having a link with them. Now with Australia being beaten by India and South Africa and losing their grip on the crown, the Australian captain if, indeed, he has been correctly quoted, is urging that the authorities should prioratise the team's scheduling and has said that IPL does not matter. Ponting, by the way, was bought for $3,50,000 or so and doesn't seem to have any Indian endorsements at the moment. Maybe that tells a story about why the recent story.

23.01.2009

aptain
a Singh Dhoni
us skipper Ricky
Australian
per Brad
Dhoni walking
e his dismissal;
land skipper
ettori.

TO WALK or Not To

There were two separate incidents involving wicketkeepers in different parts of the world that probably tells a tale of how different attitudes and approaches to playing an international game are, in different parts of the cricketing world.

In Sri Lanka, Mahendra Singh Dhoni, the captain of the Indian team did not wait for the umpire's decision and walked off the field when he was caught down the leg-side by the Sri Lankan wicketkeeper. The umpire did not hear the knick and so wasn't raising his finger, which is understandable in the subcontinent, where with the noise level it is not always easy to hear faint knick. In Sri Lanka, the music goes on non-stop, so it's very tough to hear anything if it's at some distance, and maybe the umpire didn't hear the knick nor saw any big deflection and so kept his finger by his side. At that stage India was in trouble and Dhoni was the last recognised batsman at the crease and the team were hoping that the skipper in the last seven overs would get them to a decent score. So there was every reason for Dhoni to wait for the umpire to make the decision but he opted to walk.

Today there are very few players who walk when they know they are out, believing that someday they will get a bad decision and be given out when they are not out and so they wait for the umpire to give his decision. It all evens out, is what the popular saying is though ask any batsman and he will vouch that they get more bad ones than good ones. It is no longer a moral issue but an individual choice and since just about every player prefers to wait for the umpire to make his call, a player who does not wait is a rarity, and stands out and looks so refreshing. There is no doubt that the cricketing world accepts that it is ok to wait for the umpire whose job it is to decide but when a batsman who is out, stays on and goes to score a big knock then the opposition is not amused. The obvious way to show that disapproval is not to applaud the batsman when he reaches individual landmarks such as a 50 or a 100. Not that the batsman gives a damn because he knows when the dust is settled and the history of the game is written its only the score and not how he got that or if he was fortunate that the umpire didn't rule him out when he was out.

This is about batsmen, but what about fielders who appeal for a catch when

Australian wicketkeeper Brad Haddin was accused of cheating during an ODI against New Zealand; Australian vice-captain Michael Clarke also faced a similar allegation.

they know the batsman hasn't touched the ball and when they know that they have taken the catch on the bounce. With television cameras being so good today, it is virtually impossible for a fielder to appeal for a catch when the ball has bounced but as batsmen who wait, do they too ease their conscience by saying that the batsman was out sometime earlier in the innings or even in the series and so they can take a chance and ask the umpire. In such a scenario, the feelings generated is higher than when the batsman is waiting when he knows he is out caught.

So we come to the second incident, which generated a lot of copy and finger wagging. New Zealand and Australia contests are extremely tense affairs since there is no love lost between the two countries in most matters of sport. The Aussies treat the Kiwis as kid brothers and so the Kiwis are always keen to beat them and win the bragging rights. The first One-day game at Perth was a low-scoring one. The Aussies were dismissed for less than 200 and the Kiwis struggled to get there. However, a partnership was developing when the incident occurred that caused so much anguish down under. Neil Broom and Ross Taylor were repairing the innings and slowly taking the visitors to their lowly target.

Michael Clarke, who, his skipper Ponting believes, has a golden arm and takes wickets when Australia badly needs them, got Broom to attempt a cut shot. It was the extra bounce of the Perth pitch that took the ball just above the stumps but it was the gloves of Brad Haddin that caused all the trouble. He had them in front of the stumps as he collected the ball and then in the act of gathering the ball the bails were broken. The batsman who had seen the whole incident wasn't happy that the umpire ruled him out and slow motion replays clearly showed that the ball didn't hit the stumps and the gloves were in front of the stumps. After the game which New Zealand won off the last ball and with just one wicket remaining, the Kiwi skipper in his interaction with the media suggested that he expected the wicket keeper to realise what he had done and should not have appealed. At no stage did Vettori call Haddin 'a cheat' but Ponting, when asked for his reaction to Vettori's statement that Haddin shouldn't have appealed, said that basically Haddin was being called a cheat and as usual he backed his player. Haddin, who by now had had ample time to see the incident in slow motion and realise what had happened, then had the cheek to say what Vettori had said was 'low and poor'. It is evident that he felt that what he had done was high and rich. This, by the way, is the same keeper who threw his glove at the ball when it was going past him in a Test match in India.

Two incidents involving keepers and two totally different attitudes; one is anything to win a game and the other where the skipper was sending a message to his team that yes 'we want to win but not at the cost of good sportsmanship'. Incidentally, India went on to win the match despite Dhoni's call to leave when he knew he was out. I know which attitude I would prefer. What about you?

06.02.2009

*...que Allan
...Stanford with
...n Richards;
...an great: Sir
...chere, Michael
... Clive Lloyd
...wder Joel*

ACCIDENT Waiting to Happen

The unravelling of the Allan Stanford business empire may have come as a shock to the officials of the West Indies Cricket Board, and the England and Wales Cricket Board, but to most others it was an accident waiting to happen. When an individual, howsoever rich he may be has ideas of having a tournament named after him by financing it with his companies' funds, then there is always some room for doubt and in Stanford's case, right from the start when he came to Antigua and started to invest in that lovely tiny island, there were many who refused to get swayed by his money power. Michael Holding, the great West Indian fast bowler and a super commentator, was one of those who realised very early that there was more to Stanford than what met the eye. He resigned from the Board that Stanford had set up to advise him on how to get mileage out of cricket and how his money could be best utilised for developing the sport in the West Indies. This Board consisted of the greatest of West Indian cricketers including Sir Everton Weekes, Sir Garfield Sobers, Sir Viv Richards, Clive Lloyd, Wes Hall, Joel Garner to name a few and they were all on a handsome retainer per year. Stanford did pump some much needed funds into West Indies Cricket and that bought him the confidence of those who ran West Indies Cricket. So, when he proposed a Twenty Twenty tournament between the winner of the team visiting the West Indies that year and West Indies, to play against his All Stars team for a purse of US 20 million dollars, the West Indies Board gave it its backing despite the fact that it was a private promoter who was proposing it.

That proposal, backed by the West Indies Cricket Board, was on the ICC table for the past few years. It wasn't getting through simply because the majority of the ICC Test member countries were wondering how they would get a share of the prize money offered, since Stanford had made it clear that it was a 'winner take all' contest and if his own team the Stanford All Stars won, then they would keep the 20 million. He was, of course, ready to pay an appearance fee to the Boards whose teams would be playing in the contest. The main argument of the majority of the member countries was that apart from Australia, England and India, no other team would get invited for the event simply because they were not big box office draws. So the benefit, if any, would be to only those three countries. Being a businessman,

A match progresses at the Stanford 20-20 Cup; (Inset) Sir Allan Stanford with the winning team.

Stanford knew that he would not be able to sell other teams to TV networks and so he would not be able to recover the money he was putting in the contest. Stanford even got the members of his advisory Board to meet with ICC officials in South Africa when the ICC T20 World Cup was played, but he wasn't able to sway the doubters because of his stubbornness in refusing to play for anything less than the 20 million prize money. As he proudly proclaimed, it is Twenty Twenty for Twenty.

When the Indian Premier League took off in a spectacular manner, Stanford realised that he would be marginalised and so with the West Indies Cricket Board already in his pocket, he approached the England and Wales Cricket Board. The ECB were at loggerheads with the BCCI because it perceived the lessening of its importance and the growing clout of the BCCI. It had already banned its players from playing in the IPL and it was planning an English Premier League of its own to rival the IPL. So without even thinking of the other member countries of the ICC who had steadfastly refused to be a party to the Stanford deal, the ECB went and signed a five-year deal with Stanford where its team would play against the

Stanford All Stars. Stanford by now had perhaps realised that the Twenty Twenty for Twenty was not going to work, so although he did pledge 20 million, it was split up with three and half million each to the West Indies and England Cricket Boards and the remaining was the prize money to be won. How he still managed to convince the media to call it Twenty Twenty for Twenty is a mystery because it was in reality only for 13 million and not 20. The deception was hardly noticed by the world's media and they still persisted in calling it a game for a prize of 20 million.

He flew down in a helicopter to the Lords Cricket Ground where the 20 million was displayed to the British media in the presence of former England and West Indian skippers as well as officials of both Boards. He was lucky, of course, that he was not stopped as he helicoptered into Lords simply because Lords still has not got sky marshalls to ask for valid passes to enter the ground. There again, nobody asked him why 20 million cash was being displayed when the game was for 13 million.

The ECB, on a high after its deal with Stanford, thumbed its nose at BCCI and even refused to be a founding member of the Champions League which could have earned it around 100 million a year. The Stanford deal was to get the ECB seventeen and half million over five years. Who did the maths there to refuse the chance of being a founder member of the Champions League and earn a possible 500 million over the same period, is anybody's guess but no doubt the answers will be demanded by the media especially now that the Test is drawn and there is some time before the next Test starts.

It will be interesting to see the footwork of the ECB now.

20.02.2009

Sunil 'Sunny' Gavaskar is the idol of millions the world over. His magic with the bat created several records and won the hearts of as many. Even his severest critics had to concede that he was indeed the 'Little Master'!

His transition from a cricketer to being a critic and a columnist, whom the entire media hankers after, has indeed been a welcome one. As he celebrates his sixtieth birthday, there could be no better tribute than an anthology of 'sixty' of Sunil Gavaskar' best articles. They reflect the man and are like him – 'no holds barred'! He minces no words and says it like it is. He talks about the greats of yesteryears, his heroes that include the late M.L. Jaisimha and Don Bradman amongst other. He talks about what ails the cricketing world and also how the Indian cricket team is truly a force to reckon with.

Straight Drive is timeless, quite like the man, and is a must read for all die-hard fans of Sunil Gavaskar.

Rupa • Co

ISBN 978-81-291-1753-3

9 788129 117533

Anthology   ₹ 195

www.rupapublications.com

Cover Design: PealiDezine

www.ingramcontent.com/pod-product-compliance
Lightning Source LLC
Chambersburg PA
CBHW030247070526
44654CB00045B/944